How to Talk to Families About Child and Adolescent Mental Illness

Diane T. Marsh and Melissa J. Marks

W. W. Norton & Company, Inc.
New York • London

A Part of the How to Talk Series

For information about permission to reproduce selections from this book, write to Permissions, W. W. Norton & Company, Inc., 500 Fifth Avenue, New York, NY 10110

For information about special discounts for bulk purchases, please contact W. W. Norton Special Sales at specialsales@wwnorton.com or 800-233-4830

Manufacturing by R. R. Donnelley Harrisonburg
Book design by Bytheway Publishing Services
Production manager: Leeann Graham

Library of Congress Cataloging-in-Publication Data
Marsh, Diane T.
   How to talk to families about child and adolescent mental illness /
Diane T. Marsh and Melissa J. Marks.
      p. cm. — (How to talk series)
   "A Norton professional book."
   Includes bibliographical references and index.
   ISBN 978-0-393-70570-6 (pbk.)
   1. Mentally ill children.   2. Parents of mentally ill
children—Services for.   3. Families of the mentally ill—Services for.
4. Mentally ill children—Family relationships.   5. Mentally ill
children—Care.   I. Marks, Melissa J.   II. Title.
   RJ499.M285 2009
   618.92'89–dc22   2009014097

ISBN: 978-0-393-70570-6 (pbk.)

W. W. Norton & Company, Inc., 500 Fifth Avenue, New York, N.Y. 10110
                        www.wwnorton.com
W. W. Norton & Company Ltd., Castle House, 75/76 Wells Street, London W1T 3QT

1 2 3 4 5 6 7 8 9 0

How to Talk to Families About Child and Adolescent Mental Illness

To the many children, adolescents, and family members who are coping with mental illness, thank you for teaching us about courage, commitment, and resilience.

To our own families, thank you for your love, support, and inspiration.
Diane T. Marsh
Melissa J. Marks

Special appreciation is expressed to my sister, Wendy Firestone, a dedicated school psychologist, for her insights and assistance.
M.J.M.

Contents

Preface

Our goal in writing *How to Talk to Families About Child and Adolescent Mental Illness* was to provide a comprehensive and practical resource for mental health and educational professionals who work with families who include a child or adolescent with mental illness. The challenges that confront these families are considerable. A single knowledgeable and caring practitioner can make a significant difference in their lives, helping them acquire the essential knowledge, skills, and attitudes that can empower them in meeting the needs of their child and family.

We bring a wide range of experiences to the writing of this book. Both of us are professors at the University of Pittsburgh at Greensburg. Diane T. Marsh, PhD, is a licensed psychologist with many years of experience as a university teacher, therapist, consultant, and trainer. She has written many professional books and other publications, largely concerned with family issues in mental illness. Melissa J. Marks, EdD, has taught in the public schools as well as the university, and she currently trains child psychiatrists to work with schools in meeting the needs of students with mental health problems.

Our focus is on severe and persistent mental disorders of childhood and adolescence, including anxiety disorders, depression, bipolar disorder, and schizophrenia. We provide the information that families need about these mental disorders and their treatment, the mental health and educational systems, essential coping strategies, potential home- and school-based interventions, and planning for the future. We also discuss the skills that families need to cope with the mental illness and its consequences for their family, for dealing with multiple child-serving systems, and for enhancing the quality of their lives.

Throughout the book, the voices of children and families are heard, based on their personal accounts and interviews. With power and eloquence, they share their experiences with mental illness and offer suggestions for others who are embarking on similar journeys. Their voices attest to the many challenges that accompany a diagnosis of mental illness in our society. But, their stories also document their resilience and offer ample reason for hope. Although many of these experiential quotes are from real people, the vignettes that begin Chapters 4, 5, and 7 through 12 are not actual families, but rather composites that reflect the experiences of legions of families dealing with child and adolescent mental illness on a daily basis.

We mention many publications that can provide useful information for families, but we do not duplicate material that is easily available elsewhere, such as the extensive lists of resources for families that are included in many of these publications. Some Web sites are also very helpful for families, including those of government agencies such as the Substance Abuse and Mental Health Services Administration (SAMHSA) and the National Institute of Mental Health (NIMH), those of advocacy organizations such as the National Alliance on Mental Illness (NAMI) and Mental Health America, and those of professional groups such as the American Academy of Child & Adolescent Psychiatry (AACAP), which offers a "Facts for Families" series. Because these Web sites are constantly updated and expanded, we provide the uniform resource locator (URL) rather than information about date of retrieval. On the other hand, we use standard reference format for books, journal articles, and other publications, including Web-based research reports and family guides.

IMPACT OF MENTAL ILLNESS ON CHILDREN, ADOLESCENTS, AND FAMILIES

CHAPTER ONE

Introduction

After a serious suicide attempt at her high school, Rebecca experienced her first psychiatric hospitalization. It was then that I was told if I took Rebecca home from the hospital, she would kill herself. This was the start of our nightmare. Rebecca's symptoms were now unmanageable and dangerous. I was expected to make decisions about my daughter's care at a time when I was least equipped emotionally to make decisions. I was also more isolated from my family, I had no friends, and I was more blamed by the professionals than ever before. Alone, I decided what medications to approve for Rebecca to take, which treatment programs she would attend or live in and what schools for the severely emotionally disturbed she would attend. I made decisions without any information because I had no other choice, and I made some bad decisions. I was terrified most of the time.

—Hawkins & Hawkins, p. 12

These are the words of Pam Hawkins, whose daughter Rebecca was diagnosed with bipolar disorder at age 15. We have written *How to Talk to Families About Child and Adolescent Mental Illness* to enhance professional practice with families like the Hawkins, who are often isolated, poorly informed, confused, and overwhelmed. In their joint account (Hawkins & Hawkins, 2000, pp. 11-13), Pam and Rebecca described the devastating impact of mental illness on their family, their frustrating experiences with the mental health and educational systems, and eventually their ability to manage the illness and move on with their lives. In this chapter, we hear Rebecca's story, written in her own words.

The experiences and concerns of the Hawkins family are shared by the legions of families coping with the mental illness of a child or adolescent, often with little support. A single knowledgeable and caring practitioner can make a significant difference in the lives of these often-desperate families. Our book is designed to help child and adolescent mental health and educational professionals build on their existing competencies, enhance their effectiveness in working with these families, and empower families to deal with the challenges they face.

The Scope of the Problem

The Substance Abuse and Mental Health Services Administration (SAMHSA, http://mentalhealth.samhsa.gov/) estimates that at least one in five children and adolescents have a mental health disorder. About 6 million young people—at least 1 in 10—have a serious emotional disturbance that significantly disrupts their daily functioning at home, in school, or in the greater community. Moreover, although half of all lifetime cases of diagnosable mental illness begin by age 14, fewer than one in five of these children receive the mental health services they need. As former Surgeon General David Satcher wrote in the foreword to the *Report of the Surgeon General's Conference on Children's Mental Health: A National Action Agenda* (U.S. Department of Health and Human Services [USDHHS], 2000), "a health crisis has been created in the country by the burden of suffering experienced by children with mental health needs and their families."

The price of this neglect is immeasurable for these young people, for their families, and for a society that is deprived of their contributions. When left untreated, childhood mental health disorders can lead to failure in school, family conflict, substance abuse, violence, and suicide. The *Chartbook on Mental Health and Disability in the United States* (Jans, Stoddard, & Kraus, 2004) reported that more than half of all youth with emotional disturbance drop out of school—the highest rate among all disability categories. Young patients with mental illness are at high risk for suicide. According to the American Association of Suicidology (http://www.suicidology.org/), suicide is the third leading cause of death among young people ages 15 to 24. Each day, there are approximately 12 youth suicides; for every completed suicide, an estimated 100 to 200 attempts are made. Suicide rates for children aged 10 to 14 increased 51% between 1981 and 2004.

Terminology

As indicated in our title, *How to Talk to Families About Child and Adolescent Mental Illness,* our focus is on both children and adolescents. Unless we are specifically talking about adolescents, however, we use the term *children* to refer to all those under age 18. We also use the term *families* rather than parents, although many professional contacts are with mothers and fathers. But families have changed, and the definition of family has become more fluid (Watson, 2007). Increasingly, practitioners are working with other primary caregivers, including stepparents, grandparents, other extended family members, domestic partners, foster parents, guardians, and others who have a commitment to a particular child. Accordingly, when we do mention parents, we are also referring to other primary caregivers. The principles of effective family-focused care apply to all of these caregivers.

We use the term *mental illness* to refer to serious mental, behavioral, and emotional disorders in children because the term is widely understood and conveys the severity of the disorders covered in the book. Other terms are also applicable to varying degrees, including *early-onset mental illness, serious emotional disturbance* (used by SAMHSA), *emotional disturbance* (used in special education), *serious mental illness* (used for severe and persistent disorders among adults), and *mental disorders*, which is used in the current edition of the *Diagnostic and Statistical Manual of Mental Disorders, DSM-IV-TR* (American Psychiatric Association, 2000). Still other terms, such as *mental health problems* or *mental health issues*, fail to convey the severity of such disorders as major depression, bipolar disorder, and schizophrenia.

Experiences of Children and Families

Regardless of the term, it is clear that these disorders have a profound impact on young people and their families, undermining their present lives and imperiling their future. When adolescents themselves speak of their experience with mental illness, they mention their "suffering" and "desperation"; their sense of being "marked," "invisible," and "very alone"; their awareness of "going crazy" and of being "such a disappointment"; and their "traumatic" encounters with providers (Mowbray, Megivern, & Strauss, 2002).

Their families also struggle on a daily basis. The mental illness of a child has a devastating effect on families, as one mother conveyed. "We are the parents of three little boys—one of whom has a severe mental illness," she wrote. "His illness literally took over our life, and almost destroyed us as a family" (National Alliance on Mental Illness [NAMI], 1999, p. 9). It is not just parents who are affected, but all members of the family, including siblings: "I was 16 when my 14-year-old brother had his first psychotic episode. He was hospitalized for most of my adolescence. His illness was the most devastating episode of my entire life. I was ashamed, I was afraid, I was confused" (Marsh & Dickens, 1997, p. 109).

As the first and last resort for their children, families have compelling needs of their own: for information about their child's disorder and its treatment, for skills to cope with the illness and its consequences for their family, and for support for themselves. They also need assistance navigating the mental health and educational systems. It is our hope that this book will help practitioners address the needs of these families, maximize their resilience, and support them in meeting the needs of their children. In the next chapter, we explore the family experience of childhood mental illness in more detail.

Focus on Children, Not Disorders

Although our focus is on professional practice with families, we also need to understand the experiences of the vulnerable young people who are living with mental illness. We provide essential information about specific mental disorders and their treatment, but our focus is always on children, not on diagnoses or disorders. In learning about their experiences with mental illness, we can also gain insight into the challenges faced by their families and into the mental health and educational services designed to meet their needs. At the beginning of this chapter, we heard from a parent, Pam Hawkins. Now, listen to the voices of several young people who have experienced early-onset mental illness, beginning with the account of Pam's daughter, Rebecca.

Rebecca's Journey

Rebecca Hawkins (Hawkins & Hawkins, 2000, pp. 11–13) wrote that, by the time she reached high school, she was "out of control":

> I attempted suicide and became so manic that I could throw a soft sleeper across the room without effort. I was always in some kind of fight with my mother, I wasn't attending school regularly and everything seemed frantic. This was when I was hospitalized for the first time. (p. 12)

During that hospitalization, she and her mother met with staff to discuss Rebecca's educational plans:

> They called me in and told me that I was not going back to regular school. In fact, I was told that I would never attend regular school again. It was the first time I felt really hopeless, that I was no longer a normal person. From then on I had nothing else to work on. They destroyed any hope I ever had of being a normal teenager. I became so out of control that the doctors had to medicate me to the point where I was able to do nothing but sit on the couch and drool. (p. 13)

Her mother shared Rebecca's feelings of hopelessness and helplessness. But, in fact, there was much reason for hope, as Rebecca gradually responded to treatment. At age 18, when she began advocating for better children's mental health services, she wrote that "it was empowering to finally have a voice, and to have that voice heard" (p. 13). When Rebecca wrote her personal account, she was 24 years old, living in her own apartment, working as a youth advocate, and attending college. She still has mental illness, but it is simply one aspect of her life.

Jennifer's Journey

Jennifer Martin (2000, pp. 8-10) remembers telling her mother as a child that she did not *like* school, she *loved* it. She was in the Gifted and Talented Education Program and, in the fourth grade, was elected vice president of the student council. By the time she entered high school, however, "every recognizable trace of that little girl was gone":

> By that time I was already withdrawn and displaying symptoms of depression. During my seventh and eighth grade years I experienced difficulty sleeping, poor concentration and wild appetite swings. I lost all interest in my appearance. By the time I

made it to high school, I was so depressed that simply getting out of bed was an ordeal. . . . I missed weeks of school at a time because of this. I was never reprimanded for missing so much school. When I did go to school, I went with self-inflicted cuts and welts lacing my arms. Only one teacher noticed and expressed concern for my well-being. I stopped speaking to everyone, alienating the few friends I had. The constant anxiety that gnawed at me, that had settled into a permanent home right beneath my heart began to take the form of panic attacks. (p. 8)

Jennifer spent the next year in self-imposed confinement in her home, feeling that she had been transformed into a character from the T. S. Eliot poem, one of his "hollow men":

For all intents and purposes, I fell off the face of the earth and no one noticed. I could feel my life slipping away from me. Any sense of vitality, any spark of *aliveness* that I had ever possessed was displaced. I became a pale faced wraith, a frightened bundle of inner torments incapable of handling any kind of stress. (p. 8)

Since those dark days, Jennifer has made significant progress:

By some miracle I'm here. In the last three years, I have turned my life around. I now live independently. I am a Dean's List student at a community college . . . and hope to continue at a four-year university in the fall. (p. 10)

Still, she looks back on those adolescent years with a profound sense of loss: "Sometimes I feel the loss of not only my education, but also of my youth, like a death to mourn. My life was wasted" (p. 10).

Ana's Journey

Ana Verduzco's (2000, pp. 17–20) experience as a psychiatric patient began at the age of 10, "after a couple of incidents where I acted on impulse and out of anger" (p. 17). Born in Mexico and brought to the United States by her mother as a young child, Ana's early years were troubled. Just before her 11th birthday, she was violently raped, and her "life was turned upside down" (p. 18). Ana's problems escalated over the next few years:

> I made the decision that I was done living. I had nothing to look forward to. I took my mother's gun and loaded it. I was going to shoot when I remembered my brother. What would become of him? I decided not to die yet. I did not know how to ask for help so I started cutting on my arms to relieve some of my pain. The pain in my arms held back my emotions. But as the pain in my heart and soul grew stronger, I had to take more drastic measures. I started cutting my wrist and hands. (p. 19)

One of her teachers noticed her cuts and referred her to the nurse and school psychologist. Ana was admitted to the psychiatric hospital, which was followed by other hospitalizations and placements. "I went," Ana wrote of one placement, "but without hope" (p. 19). In another placement, she was controlled with restraints, which "still haunts me to this day" (p. 19). In a large county shelter for youth who are dependents of the court, Ana endured 3 months of isolation:

> This shelter was the most traumatic of all my experiences as a psychiatric patient. . . . Remembering these months is very painful. I felt totally helpless. I was stripped of every human right. I dwelt in a dismal insanity trying to predict what cruel joke life would play on me next. (p. 20)

Like Rebecca and Jennifer, Ana has made considerable progress. She was finally discharged and resumed her outpatient treatment. At age 18, Ana wrote, "A year later, I graduated from high school where I was valedictorian. I continue receiving treatment" (p. 20).

Brandon's Journey

Brandon Fitch (1994, pp. 37–40) began to manifest symptoms of childhood schizophrenia in the second grade:

> I felt that my classmates could see through my clothes. I felt that our neighbors could see me through the windows of the house, even with the shades down. I bathed in a swimsuit, because I "knew" that the angels in heaven were looking down upon me, and wanted it that way. Faces on the covers of magazines and books watched me, too, as if they were alive. The noises in the classroom became deafening; more than I could bear. I would just get up and leave class to walk in the hallways, despite the teachers calling after me. No one understood, teachers or students. I was alone, and I cried, often. (p. 37)

As time went on, Brandon's symptoms worsened and increasingly undermined his ability to function:

> More symptoms started to afflict me; constant music playing in my head, music I could neither turn down nor drive out. I began having fleeting visual and auditory hallucinations, and struggles to make sense of my life in that scary cacophony. . . . My habits became more strange. I started wearing the same clothes every day. . . . I became intolerant and combative as I sought to avoid the stress that my small frame could barely shoulder. My moods and symptoms became exacerbated and any task seemed insurmountable. My fear of crowds, and especially teenagers, grew so great that I barely left our new apartment. I was obsessed with material objects as I sought to soothe my pain and find new distractions in the inanimate. I lived in a nether world, a sort of hellish limbo. (pp. 37–38)

Medication was tried, but with little success, and Brandon was hospitalized for the first time:

I was taken there forcibly, after attempting to throw myself out of a window. They put me in a seclusion room after being carried from the doctor's office. I resisted everything. I was terrified and was kept there for two days then released and given a gurney for a bed, and planted right in front of the nurses station, because I was so suicidal. Not only the nurses, but everybody could see this; see my shame and humiliation. Surely the world and my life were coming to an end. . . . That hospital stay became the most horrific episode of my life. The ward was dull, gray, and insulated from the outside world. The atmosphere was like a prisoner of war camp. We were observed constantly by a battery of nurses, some officious, others cold, and all seemingly incapable of caring. How does one get well here, I wondered. (pp. 38, 40)

Early-onset schizophrenia is one of the most severe and persistent mental disorders, and Brandon continued to struggle:

It seems as though, from my very beginning, I have floundered and struggled on an upstream course. My illness completely governs me and will not desist. . . . It has been a confusing and frightening world with strange perceptions and dual realities that often make no sense. . . . My top priority was just "staying alive," trying to combat the illness and maintain a tenuous hold on my sanity. . . . But, don't think for a minute that my life is an empty one, except for fantasy worlds, delusions and pills. With the illness, I have gained unique life experience. . . . When I listen to a Beethoven symphony, and understand his torment deeply, and his giftedness, my spirit soars. I read that Van Gogh, too, knew my kind of despair . . . and Munch, and so many others. And their eloquence speaks to my heart, and their humanity makes my dreams ineffably sweeter. (p. 40)

As noted in the author information accompanying his article, Brandon was featured in a *Time* magazine article about Clozaril, a newly available medication that was finally effective in controlling his symptoms. When he wrote his account at age 21, Brandon had been writing the program notes for the Cleveland Philharmonic Orchestra for 2 years.

Countering Hopelessness and Helplessness

Brandon and the other teenagers whose voices we just heard demonstrated a remarkable resilience as they learned to manage their mental illness and forge satisfying lives. But, neither they nor their families were given much reason to hope for improvement in their earlier encounters with the mental health system. In fact, for the many children and adolescents who have a severe mental illness, there is ample reason to hope for a better tomorrow.

As Ringeisen and Hoagwood (2002) affirmed, this is a time of hopeful anticipation in children's mental health. Dramatic advances in our understanding of successful strategies for the identification, diagnosis, and treatment of child and adolescent mental illness have occurred. In their review, Ringeisen and Hoagwood noted that a variety of effective interventions is now available, including psychosocial and psychopharmacological treatments, integrated community and prevention services, and school-based approaches. These interventions can successfully reduce symptoms of psychopathology, improve adaptive functioning, and sometimes serve as a buffer to further long-term impairment.

Moreover, in contrast to the past, there has been a shift toward treatment models that emphasize family inclusion and family–professional collaboration. At the same time, children's mental health has been receiving increasing attention at the highest levels of government, as shown in the groundbreaking publications, *Mental Health: A Report of the Surgeon General* (USDHHS, 1999) and the *Report of the Surgeon General's Conference on Children's Mental Health: A National Action Agenda* (USDHHS, 2000). In 2003, the New Freedom Commission on Mental Health recommended a national effort to focus on the mental health needs of young children and their families through expanded screening, assessment, intervention, training, and financing of services.

Clearly, these children, adolescents, and families represent a large and underserved population. Thus, this is an opportune time for practitioners to provide services to these vulnerable young people and their beleaguered families.

Professional Services and Practices

We examine family-focused practice in more detail elsewhere in this book. At this point, it is important to note several professional variables that can influence child and family outcomes. These include the availability of appropriate mental health and educational services, a strength-based approach to professional practice, and family–professional collaboration.

Satisfactory Mental Health and Educational Services

For families who include a child with mental illness, the first order of business is to obtain appropriate mental health and educational services. As Kazdin (2008a) noted, however, approximately 67% of the young people in need of mental health services do not receive them. The percentage is even higher among children of color and those living in rural areas. As he discussed, although numerous evidence-based psychosocial interventions are available for children, it is often difficult to obtain one of these treatments in local communities.

The problem is that our knowledge of what works with these young patients, with these disorders, and with these families is too rarely translated into clinical practice. Because the disorders discussed in the book are typically severe and persistent, with an adverse impact on multiple areas of functioning, the absence of early and effective treatment can have catastrophic long-term consequences for these young people and their families. Untreated or poorly treated, these disorders often result in suffering, disrupted lives, unfulfilled potential, isolation, shame, and lost hopes and dreams.

Regarding educational services, all children, including those with mental illness and other disabilities, are entitled to a free and appropriate public education. To meet the unique needs of children with disabilities, special education is offered through the provision of additional services, supports, programs, and specialized placements and environments. More generally, there is increasing emphasis on the development of effective and integrated school-based mental health services designed to improve the emotional well-being of students as well as their academic achievement (Kutash, Duchnowski, & Lynn, 2006).

In a policy statement regarding school-based mental health services, the American Academy of Pediatrics (2004) noted that there is great diversity in the scope of mental health services offered in the school setting. The statement described three models of service delivery: (a) school-supported mental health models, in which mental health professionals are employed directly by the school, separate mental health units exist within the school, or school nurses serve as a major portal of entry for students with mental health problems; (b) community connections models, in which services delivered by a mental health agency or individual providers are available in the school at specified times and locations or there is a formal linkage to an off-site mental health provider; and (c) comprehensive, integrated models, in which school-based health centers provide comprehensive and integrated health and mental health services within the school environment.

In Chapters 3 through 6, we discuss the mental health and educational systems in greater detail, as well as the competencies that can help families cope with these systems and with mental illness. Practitioners who can assist families to navigate the mental health and educational systems perform an invaluable service.

Strength-Based Practice

A strength-based approach to professional practice with children and families balances their strengths and resources with their limitations and deficiencies. M. D. Clark (2008) observed that there have been decades of attention devoted to how people "fall down"; it is time to advocate for the science of "getting up" and how troubled individuals and families surmount their difficulties. Indeed, many traditional models of help-giving behavior have emphasized pathology, fostered learned helplessness, increased dependency, and undermined self-esteem (Dunst, Trivette, & Deal, 1994).

In these turbulent times, as Walsh (2006) asserted, we need more than ever to understand and strengthen the ways in which families can survive and thrive. Instead of focusing on how families fail, as she reminded us, we need to direct our attention to how they succeed. What can we learn, Walsh asked, from families who build and sustain enduring relationships through difficult periods, cope effectively with an illness that cannot be cured or a problem that cannot be solved, regenerate after life-altering losses, or rise above severe trauma or the barriers of poverty and discrimination? What distinguishes healthy families is not the absence of problems but rather their ability to confront and resolve their problems as a unit. Faced with disruptive events, resilient families manage to strengthen their bonds, regain functioning, move forward with their lives, and obtain the vital resources that can help them deal with future challenges.

Family–Professional Collaboration

It is also important for professionals to establish partnerships with children, adolescents, and families. Such partnerships build on the contributions of all parties; promote an atmosphere of mutual respect; acknowledge the needs, desires, concerns, and priorities of families; involve families in decisions that affect them; and promote the development of common goals. A collaborative approach offers many benefits, including mutual engagement and satisfaction, as well as shared challenges and resources. In Chapter 11, we discuss the strategies that can promote family–professional partnerships.

Plan of the Book

Our goal in writing *How to Talk to Families About Child and Adolescent Mental Illness* was to provide a single volume designed to enhance the effectiveness of practitioners in working with families who include a child with mental illness. Throughout the book, we examine the knowledge, skills, and attitudes that can empower both therapists and families in coping with mental illness. The book is intended for child and adolescent practitioners in all mental health disciplines, including psychology, psychiatry, social work, psychiatric nursing, family therapy, and counseling. We also wrote the book for other groups, including school psychologists and other educational staff, as well as graduate students in all of these areas.

In addition to our professional audience, families themselves are likely to find the book helpful. The book will assist parents to understand the impact of early-onset mental illness on all members of the family; to acquire the knowledge, skills, and resources required to meet their child's needs; and to strengthen and support their family under challenging circumstances.

Although grounded in current thinking regarding theory, research, and practice, this book is primarily intended as an accessible and useful handbook that emphasizes clinical applications and implications. In Section I, this introductory chapter is followed by an exploration of the family experience of mental illness. Section II is designed to assist families understand and cope with the mental health and educational systems, as well as to develop essential coping skills. In Section III, specific mental disorders are discussed, including anxiety disorders, depression, bipolar disorder, and schizophrenia. Each of those chapters includes diagnostic-specific home- and school-based interventions that may be appropriate for particular children and families. In addition, those chapters include possible treatment plans as well as illustrative meetings with parents to discuss the recommended treatment plan. Section IV addresses the parameters of effective family-focused practice and family planning for the future. The disorders covered in the book are frequently severe and persistent, and families often need assistance in long-term planning.

Because the knowledge base concerned with children's mental health is expanding so rapidly, we provide general information regarding specific disorders and their effective psychosocial and psychopharmacological treatments rather than detailed information about particular interventions. Therapists working with children and families will need to provide more complete information regarding the individualized treatment plan. For professionals and families regarding evidence-based and other promising treatments for specific disorders, many resources are available, such as the National Alliance on Mental Illness (NAMI) family guide (Gruttadaro, Burns, Duckworth, & Crudo, 2007), *Choosing the Right Treatment: What Families Need to Know About Evidence-Based Practices*. Likewise, if medication is recommended, families will need detailed information about potential benefits and risks, possible side effects and complications, expected time until symptom relief, anticipated length of treatment, and other pertinent information. Many resources, including the *Physicians' Desk Reference* (published by Thomson Healthcare periodically) and pharmaceutical company Web sites, offer detailed information about medication.

CHAPTER TWO

The Family Experience
of Mental Illness

*I experienced a flood of emotions. I was shocked that this could
happen to my beautiful child. I felt fear, despair and disillu-
sionment at what might happen to my son's future. I was hor-
rified at what this meant. I was filled with pain, grief and guilt.
I felt like I was losing my son, whom I loved so very much. I
was dazed with pain and fear.*

These are the words of Janice Massie (2000, pp. 24–25), a mother
who described her reaction to the hospitalization of her son Daniel.
He was only 11 when she wrote this account. Although Daniel had
always been a "different" child, she never suspected he had a mental
illness. As his behavior worsened, however, his doctor recommended
hospitalization. Facing Daniel's admission to a locked mental health
facility, his mother wrote, "I was devastated by the reality, that there
really was something seriously wrong with my beautiful son" (p. 24).

For parents like Janice Massie, a cascade of painful emotions and
challenges accompanies the mental illness of a child. In this chapter,
based on the sizeable literature in the area and our own research, we
explore the family experience of mental illness. In the words of one

family member, "This terrible illness colors everything—a family cannot escape."

Much research has focused on families of adults with mental illness (e.g., Lefley, 1996; Marsh & Lefley, 2003), but the voices of family members resonate with similar themes throughout the lifespan, although their needs and concerns may change over time. We describe the common experiences of families who include a member with mental illness while emphasizing severe disorders of childhood and adolescence.

It is essential for professionals who work with these families to have an understanding of their reality (see Marsh & Lefley, 2009). Families are like mobiles, those unique works of art that consist of wire and colored shapes. When one member develops mental illness, it sets the family mobile in motion and affects each of its members. Indeed, for most families, mental illness is a truly transformational experience— one of those pivotal events that seem to demarcate life into "before" and "after." As family members come to terms with early-onset mental illness, clinicians can listen to their stories, provide a protected forum for the expression and resolution of painful emotions, and assist them in acquiring the knowledge and skills they need.

We begin our discussion of the family experience of mental illness with an examination of sources of family stress, both subjective and objective. Additional topics include the impact of mental illness on individual family members, family resilience, family adaptation, family diversity, and family needs.

Experiential quotations without text citations are based on interviews and surveys reported in Marsh, 1992; Marsh & Dickens, 1997; and Marsh et al., 1996.

Sources of Family Stress

Researchers and clinicians often refer to the impact of mental illness on families in terms of family or caregiver *burden*, which is the overall level of distress resulting from the illness (Lefley, 1996). Sources of family stress include the *subjective burden*, which is the personal suffering experienced by family members as a result of the illness, and the *objective burden*, which is the practical problems and hardships associated with the illness.

Subjective Burden

The subjective burden of family members often includes a painful grieving process, as well as a range of intense emotions, including shock, disbelief, anger, despair, anxiety, and shame. In this section, we discuss five components of the subjective burden: grief, depression, guilt, the "emotional roller coaster," and empathic pain.

Grief
Telling their stories, family members often speak of their feelings of grief and loss. In the words of one mother, "In the dark soul of the night, I grieve for all of us: for the anguish of the past and the present, and for the uncertainty of the future." Another mother commented, "You do grieve, not only for what your child has lost but for the many changes and demands that are made for yourself. I don't think you ever really quit grieving." Families may mourn for the child they knew before the onset of the illness, for the anguish of their family, and for their personal losses. As Rando (1986) discussed, children represent many things to parents: promise, aspirations, dreams, fantasies, and new beginnings. One mother lamented, "The sense of what might have been is overwhelming."

Depression
Responding to survey questions concerned with the impact of their child's mental illness on their own mental health (Marsh, 1992), almost all mothers (96%) said they had experienced depression in response to their child's illness. In interviews, these mothers repeatedly described symptoms of depression, including feelings of hopelessness and helplessness, decreased energy, loss of interest and pleasure in their usual

activities, feelings of worthlessness, and tearfulness. Here are the words of one mother:

> The problems with my daughter were like a black hole inside of me into which everything else had been drawn. My grief and pain were so intense sometimes that I barely got through the day. I felt as if it were a mourning process.

Guilt

Most of these mothers (87%) also reported feeling guilty. Once a diagnosis has been made, parents almost reflexively ask themselves what they have done wrong:

> I felt like a failure. I'm a single parent. All kinds of guilt went through my mind. What did I do wrong? What did I do to this child? My most precious possession in life, and I've done something wrong.

Often, this sense of guilt is exacerbated by others who assume that if there is a troubled child, the parents must be responsible. Sometimes, guilt is intensified by other family members or friends—or even strangers in a supermarket—who respond disdainfully when a child behaves inappropriately. Professionals may also intensify the guilt experienced by families, particularly if they espouse older conceptual models of family pathogenesis or dysfunction. One father described his experience with professionals who appeared to be holding him and his wife responsible for their son's mental illness: "They seemed to be trying to find out how we caused it. It was just devastating."

Emotional Roller Coaster

As their stories attest, families sometimes feel they are riding an emotional roller coaster in response to the periods of relapse and remission that typically mark the course of some severe mental disorders, including major depression, bipolar disorder, and schizophrenia. These cycles create considerable turmoil for family members, who may experience intense distress when renewed hope is shattered by another crisis or hospitalization, as the following mother conveyed: "When things are going well, you begin to hope and dream again about a better future. And when things fall apart, it is like a small death. You are more vulnerable for having dared to hope again."

Empathic Pain

In addition to their own emotional turmoil, parents may experience empathic pain for their child's distress or for the anguish experienced by other family members. Parents may be painfully aware of the discrepancy between their child's previous potential and current prospects:

> I'm just falling apart inside. Here's my daughter who's so smart. Her IQ is 140. She's written plays. She got standing ovations, and her personality just bubbled. She was in cheerleading. The teachers just loved her. And here's this kid who is so out of control that she's run away from home in the cold, she's kicking the state cop, and I've got to put her in the hospital.

Another mother conveyed her sense of foreboding about her daughter's future:

> When she went to a mental hospital, it just broke our hearts. We felt this devastation, like this is it for our child. She's never going to have a future, she's never going to have a husband and children, and she'll never have a job. Nothing will ever change.

Objective Burden

Along with the subjective burden, families experience an objective burden: the family's daily problems and challenges associated with the illness. Families must learn to cope with the symptoms of the illness, caregiving responsibilities, disruption and stress, child-serving systems, and social stigma.

Symptoms

Depending on their child's diagnosis, family members may have to cope with anxiety-related symptoms, disturbances of mood, potentially harmful or self-destructive behavior, socially inappropriate or disruptive behavior, or psychotic symptoms, such as hallucinations and delusions. Moreover, the specter of suicide is a reality for these families, whose children are far more likely to commit suicide than young people in the general population. Certainly, these symptoms present the greatest challenges for children themselves, but families also share the onus:

> My kid doesn't have a chance. There's no place that I can take him that he's not going to act up. There's nobody who understands. Nobody knows what we go through. They don't have to live here. They don't have to deal with it on a daily basis. They see you in the office once a week, once a month, whatever. They don't get a chance to see what hell it can be to live with that kid. They don't see what hell it is for the kid.

Caregiving

As Lefley (1996) discussed, to meet their child's needs, families are forced to assume roles for which they are unprepared and untrained. They must learn to cope with the requirements of daily life with a child who has mental illness, to obtain services from the mental health and educational systems, and perhaps to negotiate with other child-serving systems, such as juvenile justice or child welfare. A high price is often paid for caregiving by family members, especially mothers, who may sacrifice their own life plans. As one mother said, "My daughter's mental illness pushed us back into parenting of the most demanding kind, probably for the rest of our lives."

Family Disruption

Families often complain of high levels of stress and disruption. At least periodically, they are likely to face household disarray, financial difficulties, strained marital and family relationships, challenges to their own physical and mental health, and diminished social lives. When families experience these problems on a continuing basis, with little opportunity for respite—as many families do—exhaustion and burnout are virtually inevitable. One mother of a teenager with mental illness described her home life as "exceedingly stressful": "I'm always in the middle of arguments or on edge trying to keep a volcano from erupting."

Child-Serving Systems

Children with mental illness often require a wide range of mental health and educational services. Unfortunately, services are not always available. Indeed, as noted, at least two thirds of children and adolescents with mental disorders receive no treatment at all. When they are available, services are not always satisfactory. Even when their children receive appropriate services, professional services are often lacking for families themselves, who may report unsatisfactory handling of crises and emergencies, insufficient communication and availability on the part of professionals, and an absence of programs and services for families (Marsh, 1998). As one mother complained, "It was extremely frustrating. I felt like I was the only one who knew my kid. I was going to so many different people for help. Nobody's listening to me. How come nobody would listen to me?"

Stigma

For many families, the stigma that accompanies a diagnosis of mental illness in our society is one of the most distressing components of the family burden. Among adults with mental illness, stigma results in marginalization and ostracism; discrimination in housing, employment, and insurance; an adverse impact on all aspects of functioning; and decreased likelihood that they will receive treatment. Often internalized by individuals with mental illness and their families, negative social attitudes and expectations may result in a debilitating sense of hopelessness and helplessness, lowered self-esteem, damaged family relationships, and feelings of isolation and shame (Lefley, 1996).

Families of children with mental illness are also adversely affected by stigma, which may keep them from getting treatment and increase their sense of isolation and estrangement. One family member observed that the stigma had "translated into an internalized feeling that something is wrong with me"; another wrote of feeling like a "perpetual outsider."

Individual Family Members

Although there are universal dimensions to the family experience of mental illness, many variables mediate the impact on individual family members, including their age, gender, and role in the family. For example, the impact of the illness on individual family members partly reflects the specific developmental tasks that were disrupted by the illness, leaving a residue of "unfinished business" in its wake. In working with families, it is important to pose Rolland's (1994) essential developmental questions: What life plans have the family or individual members had to cancel, postpone, or alter? Whose plans are most and least affected?

In this section, we explore the unique experiences and concerns of parents, siblings, and extended family members, including grandparents.

Parents

Compared with other members of the family, parents—especially mothers—have had the most contact with clinicians and researchers. Thus, there is greatest understanding of their experiences and of the interventions that can address their needs. As discussed, parents share in the subjective and objective family burden. In addition to the impact on the family unit, the stress and disruption that accompany early-onset mental illness create fertile ground for marital conflict, especially at the onset of the illness.

Researchers (Taylor et al., 2000) have suggested that mothers and fathers may respond to their shared tragedy in very different ways. For decades, we have assumed that human beings respond to severe stress with a "fight-or-flight" response in which the body prepares for either aggression or hasty withdrawal. In fact, that response now appears to be more characteristic of males. When faced with a stressful event, females are more prone to a "tend-and-befriend" response, striving to protect and nurture their children and to reach out to supportive females. Thus, just as mothers are becoming engaged in the vortex of caregiving and turning to others for support, fathers may be taking flight from clamorous family demands and unmanageable emotions.

Whatever the eventual outcome, the marriage contract is inevitably renegotiated as a result of a child's mental illness. Sometimes, the illness becomes forbidden territory—an "elephant in the room"—that cannot be discussed openly. Family members may walk around the elephant and ignore its presence, thus not only blocking painful feelings and conflicts from surfacing but also preventing their resolution. Sometimes, the marriage does not survive. And sometimes, the marriage is reconstructed in fulfilling ways: "I think it's made our marriage stronger because we've shared the grief and we've shared the joys."

Siblings

The mental illness of a brother or sister has a profound impact on siblings. Siblings may mourn for their well brother or sister, for a shared past now shadowed by a painful present, and for the loss of an anticipated future with a healthy relative. As one sibling related, "To me, it was a death. The person whom I knew and was so much like me in so many ways had died, and I didn't know this person who was living in the house any more" (Goode, 1989, p. 63). Unlike a biological death, however, siblings need to adapt to an altered relationship, which can be very difficult: "I have found it almost impossible to let go of what our relationship once was and accept what our relationship has become" (Weisburd, 1992, p. 13).

Siblings often feel like forgotten family members in the wake of their brother's or sister's illness. One sibling wrote that "my brother and I felt there was no time for us; everyone was consumed by what was going on with my sister. We no longer mattered" (Kelley, 1992, p. 28). Another commented, "For many years I looked for answers for my brother's problems, never realizing I had to find myself first." Outside the family, siblings are typically ignored by a mental health system that seems impervious to their distress and concerns. Along with their parents, siblings may experience intrusions into their family life space as professionals probe every aspect of their family. Recalling her own family's experience, one sibling said she felt "like a butterfly under a microscope."

In addition, siblings may experience "survivor's guilt" simply because they have been spared mental illness themselves. Through neither of their faults, one sibling has remained well, while the other suffers from mental illness. Siblings may shoulder an irrational belief that somehow their own good mental health has been achieved at the expense of their brother or sister, a belief that can strip their life of pleasure. At the same time, siblings may assume the role of a "replacement child" who can compensate their devastated parents. An adult sibling wrote, "I became the perfect child to spare my parents more grief. But I have spent my life trying to run away from this problem. Feeling guilty and helpless, the unending sorrow for not being able to help."

Their encounter with mental illness may have an enduring impact that reverberates throughout their lives. One sibling wrote that her sister's mental illness had translated into "a pervasive sense of shame"; another remarked, "The pain and grief made it impossible for me to enjoy the 'best years' of my life." Growing up, they may feel alienated from peers: "I felt unacceptable to my peers and restricted my friendships to a few people who accepted me and did not ask too many questions." As adults, they may worry about their obligations to their brother or sister: "I worry about the present and future."

At the same time, siblings may also enjoy the gratifications that can accompany our longest relationship. One adult sibling recalled a difficult adolescence marked by a sense that her "point of reference was gone" when her older sister developed schizophrenia. Twenty years later, she and her sister have a close and fulfilling relationship: "Our relationship is great—we have the same sister feelings we had before her illness." They may also experience the satisfaction of playing a constructive role in their relative's life: "I always tried to be stable, calm, and understanding. I never forget that it could have been me."

In Chapter 6, we offer strategies for meeting the needs of well siblings, which can increase the likelihood of these positive outcomes.

Extended Family Members

The impact of mental illness on grandparents and other members of the extended family has received almost no attention from clinicians and researchers. In contrast, as Seligman and Darling (2007) discussed, there is some understanding of the impact of other childhood disabilities, such as mental retardation, on grandparents. For example, they may experience feelings of helplessness in response to the family crisis, as well as an identity crisis, because many grandparents perceive a grandchild to be an extension of themselves. In addition, grandparents often experience a dual grief as they mourn both the loss of a normal grandchild and the burden that confronts their own adult child (Fewell, 1986).

In some families, grandparents share fully in the family experience of mental illness and provide essential support for the nuclear family. In other families, grandparents and other extended family members may respond with denial, blame, and withdrawal, often because they are poorly informed. Compounding the problem, some parents may internalize the stigma that pervades the larger society and retreat behind a facade of normalcy, fearful that the "family secret" of mental illness may be revealed. One mother said, "We had been going through this problem with my son for several months. I didn't reveal this to any of my family, and we're very close. I thought, how can I tell them? I don't like to upset other people." In fact, when she did share her son's mental illness with her extended family members, they immediately came to her home to offer support.

Some other mothers who participated in our interviews shared similar experiences. One mother said that her child's grandmother "took a while to realize what was going on, but now helps in any way and tells me this all saddens her daily." Another noted the support she received from her brothers and sisters: "Even though they are many miles apart, they have been emotionally supportive. I know if I really needed any of them, they'd help me as much as they could. That means a lot to me."

Family Resilience

Because it is so well documented, family burden has come to define the family experience of mental illness in many respects. As with any major stressor, however, mental illness may serve as a catalyst for positive change in individuals and families, which is an important consideration for practitioners. Namely, the *disintegration* that often accompanies child or adolescent mental illness—the breaking down of existing patterns—offers an opportunity for constructive *reintegration* as new family adaptations and relationships are forged. Earlier in the book, we mentioned family *resilience* (e.g., Walsh, 2006), namely, the capacity of families to prevail over adversity.

We conducted a survey to learn more about the potential for family resilience in mental illness (Marsh et al., 1996). Our objective was to provide a more balanced picture of the family experience, one that acknowledges strengths as well as limitations, courage as well as despair, and resilience as well as burden. Our results provided strong evidence for personal and family resilience. In the words of one family member, "I've become a much stronger person. I'm far more compassionate and considerate toward others. Our family learned exactly what we value, and I think it's brought us even closer to each other."

When survey participants were asked if any positive family consequences resulted from the mental illness, most (88%) responded affirmatively. These relatives of people with mental illness—parents, spouses, siblings, children, grandparents, aunts, and uncles—told us about their family bonds and commitments, their expanded knowledge and skills, their advocacy activities, and their role in their relative's recovery. In the words of one sibling, "When a family experiences something like this, it makes for very compassionate people—people of substance. My brother has created a bond among us all that we will not allow to be broken." Similarly, a mother proclaimed, "We are proud that our family has remained intact and strong."

We also asked these family members whether as individuals they had experienced any positive consequences as a result of the illness. Almost all (99%) reported that they had. One wrote, "I can now say that, like that old aluminum foil ad, I am 'oven-tempered for flexible strength.'" Another asserted, "I can handle anything that comes my way. Some of the good things include a sense of pride and integrity, resourcefulness, and responsibility." These family members mentioned their greater compassion and tolerance, impressive coping skills, healthier attitudes and priorities, contributions as family members and advocates, and greater appreciation of life. In short, their transformative encounter with mental illness had created better, stronger, and more caring human beings.

Ever mindful of the burden that accompanies early-onset mental illness, practitioners also need to acknowledge the potential for resilience under the most challenging circumstances and to encourage and reinforce constructive family adaptation.

Family Adaptation

With time, most families do learn to cope. They learn about the mental illness and child-serving systems, acquire the necessary skills, and develop new sources of social support. Many professionals have described this process of family adaptation in terms of stages or phases (e.g., Spaniol & Zipple, 1997). When asked directly, most family members say they have moved through a series of phases in coming to terms with the mental illness of their child (Marsh, 1992). Although there is no single family pattern or pace of adaptation, the following phase structure provides a useful framework for understanding family adaptation to mental illness: initial encounter, confrontation, and resolution.

Initial Encounter

When first confronted with the mental illness of a child or adolescent, many family members experience feelings of shock, denial, and confusion. Their initial response is often a paralyzing sense of disbelief. With little understanding of mental illness, families may dismiss the behavior as a temporary aberration that will disappear with time or as a developmental stage. Especially during this initial phase, denial is a common response that may serve as a protective function rather than a pathological sign. When denial persists, however, it prevents children with mental illness from receiving the help they so urgently need and can preclude family members from moving on with their own lives.

Confrontation

Whatever their initial reaction to the onset of child or adolescent mental illness, eventually most family members do come to terms with the illness and its meaning for their lives. As they enter the confrontation phase, they may experience the full force of the subjective burden, including intense feelings of grief and loss; a wide range of negative emotions, including anger, guilt, depression, despair, and helplessness; preoccupation with the illness; and periodic emotional eruptions that may interfere with ongoing activities.

Resolution

During the resolution phase, families experience a gradual decline of the intense feelings experienced earlier. They are now able to understand and accept the illness. Although family members do not forget the loss, they are able to reinvest their energy in their personal and family lives. The illness is placed in perspective as a single event in the family life space. Some family members choose to join forces with other families through advocacy organizations, working for change in child-serving systems and in the larger society, which can help them gain a sense of meaning in their struggle.

One mother described the adaptation process of her family, beginning with the onset of her daughter's mental illness:

> All of a sudden, everything that had been secure and comfortable was in turmoil. There was a sense that things would never be the same again. There is painful territory now that didn't exist before, but the territory is smaller than it was, and it leaves room for the rest of my life. And our family is different now. It includes a member with mental illness, which has required major adjustments from all of us. But we have made those adjustments and are stronger and more compassionate.

Barriers to Resolution

Although most family members eventually adapt to their altered circumstances, there are many challenges along the way. As families come to terms with their child's mental illness, they rarely move smoothly through a series of phases that culminate in a state of serene acceptance. In reality, they are more likely to experience continuing feelings of grief and loss that wax and wane in response to the course of the illness or to events in their own lives. These continuing feelings have been termed *chronic sorrow* (see Marsh, 1998), which may be woven into the familial fabric on a continuing basis, with the potential for periodic emotional firestorms or a sense of shadowed lives. One mother remarked that her family had "lost its joie de vivre someplace along the way."

From the perspective of clinical practice, it is important to note that the adaptation process differs not only across families but also within them. Some family members quickly come to terms with the mental illness; others may experience prolonged grief or anger, and still others may remain in denial. This diversity is an important consideration for practitioners.

Family Diversity

Many variables can affect the family's experience of mental illness and adaptation process. Some are child variables, such as the diagnosis. As Moltz (1993) discussed, for example, mood disorders have a "contagious" quality. Namely, living with someone who is depressed is often a depressing experience. Other important variables include the characteristics of individual family members, such as their age, gender, role, personality, physical and mental health, coping effectiveness, values and beliefs, and living arrangements. Family characteristics are also important, such as their composition, social class, ethnicity, religious affiliation, life cycle issues, overall effectiveness, quality of family relationships, and other family stressors, such as unemployment or chronic health problems. Finally, the larger sociocultural context affects families, including the availability of community services for the child and family, as well as more pervasive social values, policies, attitudes, and barriers.

There has been increasing attention to ethnocultural diversity, which has an impact on the family experience of mental illness and on professional practice with families. In most important respects, the family's experience of mental illness, including the subjective and objective burden, is generalizable across groups regardless of ethnicity, race, or cultural heritage. Nevertheless, researchers have demonstrated some important differences among racial and ethnic groups (Lefley, 1998). For example, many ethnic minority families find mainstream mental health services alien to their cultural values and traditions. As a result, these families may choose not to seek services, may terminate services prematurely, or may find treatment unhelpful (Kazdin, Stolar, & Marciano, 1995). In response, providers are beginning to design programs especially for ethnic minority families (Finley, 1997).

Family Needs

As a result of child or adolescent mental illness, families have a number of essential needs themselves (see Marsh, 1998, 2001). In addition to their need for satisfactory services for their young family member, these highly stressed families need information about their child's mental illness, its treatment, and available services; about skills to cope with the illness and its consequences for their family; and about support for themselves. We talk in other chapters about the many ways professionals can assist these families to meet their needs. Once families have acquired the information, skills, and support they so urgently need under these circumstances, they will be better able to cope with the mental illness and to create a nurturing environment for all of their members, with outcomes such as the following:

> My husband once asked me how it was possible that I evolved unscathed from my upbringing with a brother who has mental illness. It never occurred to me that as a family we should have fallen apart. It was simple—you love your family, you care for each individual, you respect each other. It always felt solid, it felt right.

HELPING FAMILIES COPE WITH MENTAL ILLNESS

CHAPTER THREE

Helping Families Cope With the Mental Health System

Funds ran out because my daughter had spent a lot of time in the inpatient unit of the community mental health center before she went to the hospital. The hospital was in another county. Our county wouldn't pay for her being in the other county, and our insurance paid $10,000 lifetime for this kind of illness. So when it was all used up, all the tests stopped, everything was forgotten, and it was, "We have to get this child out of here as fast as possible." When the state hospital didn't have any more funds from the county to take care of her, they said she has to go.

As this mother attested, the mental health system presents many challenges for families trying to obtain appropriate services for a child or adolescent, particularly if the mental illness is severe and persistent, as it was for this teenager. Especially in their early encounters with the system, families may feel that they are dealing with a maze rather than a coherent system. This mother was interviewed more than a decade ago. Although the mental health system continues to pose problems for families, the intervening years have witnessed many changes to the child service system, with many more on the horizon.

Indeed, the final report of the New Freedom Commission on Mental Health (2003) called for a transformed mental health system and asserted that enhanced treatment for children and adolescents is a strategic investment that will create long-term benefits for individuals, systems, and society as a whole. Practitioners can offer a valuable service by explaining the evolving mental health system to families and helping them navigate their way through it. In the opening vignette in Chapter 1, Pam Hawkins lamented, "I made decisions without any information because I had no other choice, and I made some bad decisions." Our goal is to assist family members like Pam to obtain the information they need to make informed decisions about programs, services, and treatments.

This system transformation includes the development of effective and integrated school-based mental health services, which are discussed in Chapters 4 and 5. In this chapter, we examine the mental health system; the system-of-care model, programs, and services; the evaluation process; treatment; and professional roles and responsibilities. Families need information about all of these topics. Given this array of information, however, it is no wonder that families often feel overwhelmed and confused by their encounters with the mental health system. Accordingly, the final section discusses resources and strategies that can assist families to navigate the mental health maze.

The Mental Health System

We begin with an overview of the mental health system. In fact, as discussed in the surgeon general's report on mental health (U.S. Department of Health and Human Services [USDHHS], 1999), what is sometimes called the *de facto mental health service system* is really a network of diverse, relatively independent, and loosely coordinated facilities and services that provide treatment for mental health problems. As discussed in the report, the mental health system is usually described as having four major components or sectors: (a) the specialty mental health sector, which consists of mental health professionals such as psychiatrists, psychologists, and social workers; (b) the general medical or primary care sector, which consists of health care professionals such as pediatricians and family physicians; (c) the human services sector, which consists of social services, school-based counseling services, and services in the child welfare and juvenile justice systems; and (d) the voluntary support network sector, which consists of advocacy and self-help groups, such as the National Alliance on Mental Illness (NAMI; http://www.nami.org/) and Mental Health America (http://www.nmha.org/), which offer educational programs, support groups, and other services.

To further complicate matters for families, as the report indicated (USDHHS, 1999), the mental health system is divided into private and public sectors. The term *private sector* refers to services directly operated by private agencies and to services financed with private resources, such as employer-provided insurance. The term *public sector* refers to services operated by government agencies, such as state and county mental hospitals, and to services financed with government resources, such as Medicaid, a federal–state program for financing health care services for people who are poor and disabled, as well as special programs for children with serious emotional disturbance.

The public sector is designed to serve individuals with no health insurance or those who exhaust mental health benefits in their health insurance. When mental health problems are severe and persistent—as they typically are for the disorders discussed in this book—families may need to access services from each service component and from both public and private sectors of the mental health system. For instance, families who initially access private mental health care using health insurance may turn to the public sector when their lifetime benefits are reached. With the passage of federal mental health parity legislation in 2008, health insurance coverage for mental disorders must be equal to that provided for medical and surgical care, but repeated hospitalizations can still exhaust lifetime benefits.

Children and adolescents with mental illness often have problems in several functional domains and require services from multiple child-serving systems, including the mental health, educational, child welfare, juvenile justice, substance abuse, and primary health care systems. Moreover, they often need long-term care, multidisciplinary approaches to intervention, and a wide range of services beyond therapy and medication. Because traditional managed care plans generally do not cover many of these services, young people and their families are best served by an integrated and coordinated multidisciplinary service system, namely, by a *system of care*.

A System of Care

The Substance Abuse and Mental Health Services Administration (SAMHSA, 2007) has defined a *system of care* as a coordinated network of community-based services and supports that are organized to meet the challenges of children and adolescents with serious mental health needs and their parents. These young people and their families work in partnership with public and private organizations to design mental health services and supports that are effective, that build on the strengths of individuals and families, and that address each person's cultural and linguistic needs. A system of care assists children and families to improve functioning in home, in school, in the community, and throughout life. A system of care is not a program; rather, it is a philosophy of how care should be delivered. This model recognizes the importance of family, school, and community and promotes the potential of children by addressing their physical, emotional, intellectual, cultural, and social needs.

Multidisciplinary and interagency teams facilitate cross-system coordination and collaboration by working with individual families, including the young person, as partners when developing a service plan and making decisions affecting care. Team members may include family advocates as well as representatives from relevant child-serving systems and perhaps other community agencies or organizations. The teams focus on the strengths of the youth and the family rather than solely on their problems. As Pires (2002) discussed, the goal is to move from fragmented to coordinated service delivery; from limited services to a comprehensive service array; and from reactive, crisis-oriented services to prevention and early intervention.

As specified by SAMHSA (2007), several core values characterize systems of care, which are child centered, family focused and family driven, community based, and culturally competent and responsive. Reflecting the guiding principles, services should be individualized and comprehensive, incorporating a broad array of services and supports; focused on early identification and intervention; provided in the least-restrictive clinically appropriate settings; integrated and coordinated through a designated care manager; and planned to offer smooth transitions to adult services.

There is empirical support for the effectiveness of the system-of-care model. As SAMHSA (2007) reported, research findings suggest that effective systems of care reduce the number of costly hospital and out-of-home residential treatment placements, improve the behavior and emotional functioning of children and adolescents, improve school performance, reduce violations of the law, and provide services to more individuals and families who need them. Thus, the system-of-care approach not only helps children thrive in their homes and communities but also is a wise investment of scarce resources.

A Continuum of Care

Because children with mental illness have service needs that are often unmet by traditional outpatient treatment, practitioners need to be familiar with the array of services, programs, and interventions that may be offered to these families. A complete range of services and programs is called a *continuum of care*. Most communities provide only some programs and services, although some psychiatric hospitals and other organized systems of care provide many of the services on the continuum.

Programs and Services

As part of their "Facts for Families" series, the American Academy of Child & Adolescent Psychiatry (2004; http://www.aacap.org/) offers a brief description of the following programs and services:

- The office or outpatient clinic, which typically offers visits of 30 to 60 minutes; the number of visits depends on the child's needs;
- Intensive case management, in which specially trained individuals coordinate or provide mental health, financial, legal, and medical services to help the child live successfully at home and in the community;
- Home-based treatment services, in which a team of specially trained staff go into a home and develop a treatment program to help the child and family;
- Family support, which provides services such as parent training, a parent support group, and the like to help families care for their child;
- Partial hospitalization (day hospital), which provides all the treatment services of a psychiatric hospital, but the patients return home each evening;
- Emergency/crisis services, which provide 24-hour services for emergencies, such as those of a hospital emergency room or mobile crisis team;
- Respite care services, by which the child stays briefly away from home with specially trained individuals;
- The therapeutic group home or community residence, which usually includes 6 to 10 children per home and may be linked with a day treatment program or specialized educational program;
- The crisis residence, which provides short-term (usually fewer than 15 days) crisis intervention and treatment with 24-hour supervision;
- The residential treatment facility, which provides youth with serious mental illness intensive and comprehensive mental health treatment in a campus-like setting on a longer-term basis; and

• Hospital treatment, which offers comprehensive mental health treatment in a hospital that is specifically designed to treat either children or adolescents.

The Evaluation Process

Once families have entered the mental health system, their child is likely to undergo an evaluation process. Initially, a comprehensive evaluation is undertaken to identify the problems of the child, to determine the diagnosis, to make recommendations for treatment, and to develop an individualized treatment plan. Depending on the agency and the treatment team, the evaluation may be conducted by a child and adolescent psychiatrist, by a clinical psychologist, or by a team of mental health professionals. Families often benefit from a discussion of psychiatric and psychological evaluations so they can understand and prepare for the evaluation process and can bring information that may be needed. They should also be informed that a diagnosis might be required for insurance reimbursement and treatment planning.

As described by the American Academy of Child & Adolescent Psychiatry (2005; http://www.aacap.org/), a psychiatric evaluation is conducted by a child or adolescent psychiatrist and may require several hours over one or more office visits with the child and parents. With the permission of the parents, other significant people may be contacted, such as the family physician, school personnel, or other relatives. The evaluation frequently includes the following:

• Description of present problems and symptoms;
• Information about the child's medical and psychiatric history;
• Information about the family's medical and psychiatric history;
• Information about the child's development;
• Information about family relationships;
• Information about school and friends;
• An interview with the child or adolescent;

- An interview with the parents or guardians; and,
- If needed, laboratory studies, such as blood tests, or special assessments, such as educational or speech and language evaluations.

Following the evaluation, the psychiatrist develops a formulation that describes the child's problems, provides a specific diagnosis, and offers recommendations.

A psychological evaluation is generally performed by a licensed psychologist, who covers the same issues addressed in the psychiatric evaluation and provides similar conclusions and recommendations. In addition, the psychologist usually administers a battery of tests to assess the functioning of the child in various domains. Depending on the presenting problem, in a 2-hour session the psychologist might administer some combination of tests that measure intelligence, academic achievement, psychosocial functioning, and neuropsychological functioning as well as tests that target specific disorders, such as depression, or that screen for a wide range of mental disorders. In addition, psychologists may also ask parents (and sometimes teachers) to complete checklists or inventories.

When several members of a treatment team evaluate a child, the roles and responsibilities of professionals are complementary and cover the topics mentioned under the psychiatric evaluation. In a given setting, for example, a psychiatrist might determine the diagnosis, a psychologist might administer several tests, a social worker might evaluate the family circumstances, and the treatment team might develop the service plan.

Treatment

Intervention is a broad concept that encompasses many different methods designed to assist troubled children and their families. The intervention spectrum includes prevention, treatment, and aftercare.

Treatment refers to strategies that are used to eliminate or reduce the symptoms of a mental disorder.

Following the evaluation, an individualized treatment plan will be formulated that reflects the unique characteristics and mental health problems of the child, the child's circumstances, and the family. Although treatment plans vary across agencies and among clinicians, the plans usually include a behavioral problem definition (behavioral manifestations based on the text revision of the *Diagnostic and Statistical Manual of Mental Disorders, Fourth Edition* [*DSM-IV-TR*] American Psychiatric Association, 2000); long-term goals designed to resolve presenting problems; short-term objectives that target each behavioral problem; and therapeutic interventions designed to accomplish the short-term objectives. Also included are a *DSM-IV-TR* diagnosis and a treatment plan review date.

Families will need detailed information about their child's diagnosis and the interventions recommended in the treatment plan. That diagnostic-specific information is provided in Chapters 7 through 10. Families also benefit from general information about evidence-based practice (EBP), psychosocial interventions, and psychopharmacological interventions. In this chapter, we offer a brief overview of those topics.

Evidence-Based Practice

As Kazdin (2008b) discussed, *evidence-based treatment* (EBT) refers to the interventions or techniques that have produced therapeutic change in controlled studies. *Evidence-based practice* (EBP) is a broader term that refers to clinical practice that is informed by evidence about interventions, clinical expertise, and patient needs, values, and preferences and that is integrated into decision making about individual care. As he observed, one concern of professionals—and of families—is the proliferation of new child and adolescent treatments. Over 550 treatments are now available, and the number continues to increase. Thus, information about what works with specific disorders is essential for treatment planning.

An excellent guide for families, *Choosing the Right Treatment: What Families Need to Know About Evidence-Based Practice* was published by NAMI (Gruttadaro et al., 2007). As the guide pointed out, there is no substitute for a comprehensive evaluation to determine the individual needs of each child and family. This evaluation should lead to a choice of interventions that support a child's goals, build on strengths, and enhance problem-solving and coping skills. Ideally, as discussed, a range of treatment options should be available.

Although information on EBT is important, it should not be the sole consideration. Many EBTs are currently available in only a limited number of communities. In addition, other promising interventions are available that do not yet have the empirical support to be considered EBTs. There may also be other reasons why families might consider an intervention with limited evidence, such as the prior failure of EBTs, the unique circumstances of the child and family, or conflict with the family's cultural values and beliefs.

Psychosocial Interventions

Many resources that describe child and adolescent psychosocial interventions are available for professionals and families. The NAMI family guide (Gruttadaro et al., 2007) provides a useful list of current EBTs in children's mental health. Some are designed to treat the disorders covered in this book; others are intended for different problems and populations, such as juvenile offenders. Because young people often have problems in multiple domains, we provide brief descriptions of each EBT:

- Cognitive-behavioral therapy (CBT), which teaches children how to identify and change negative or maladaptive thoughts and behavior that have an impact on their feelings;

- Exposure therapy, which assists children to manage fears by gradually exposing them to threatening situations, thoughts, or memories;
- Interpersonal therapy (IPT), which is designed to treat depression by examining relationships and transitions and how they affect thoughts and feelings;
- Behavior therapy, which helps children change maladaptive behavior through a reward-and-consequence system;
- Brief strategic family therapy (BSFT), which focuses on improving the interactions between the child and family;
- Functional family therapy (FFT), which is designed to engage families in decreasing problems in their family, such as school dropout or juvenile offending;
- Parent management training (PMT), which helps parents develop effective child behavior management skills for reducing difficult and disruptive behaviors;
- Parent–child interaction therapy (PCIT), which assists parents to address their child's challenging and disruptive behaviors;
- Family psychoeducation, which is designed to offer education about early-onset mental illness and its treatment, to strengthen coping skills, and to support family members (psychoeducation is an EBT in adult mental health for such disorders as bipolar disorder and schizophrenia);
- Wraparound services, which include a definable planning process that involves the child and family in accessing an individualized set of community services and natural supports;
- Multisystemic therapy (MST), which provides short-term and intensive home-based therapy designed to treat disruptive behavior disorders, such as conduct disorders;
- Treatment foster care (TFC), which provides a placement outside the family for the treatment of serious mental health problems, including disruptive behavior disorders;
- Mentoring programs, in which adults help young people increase their healthy activity and involvement in school and community; and

• Respite care, which is a type of family support that provides relief from child care by bringing a caregiver into the home or placing a child in another setting for a brief period of time.

Psychopharmacological Interventions

There has been a steady increase in the use of psychotropic medications to treat children and adolescents with mental illness. Medication, which may be appropriate if the symptoms are severe and disabling or if other treatments have been ineffective, is generally prescribed in combination with psychosocial interventions. As the NAMI guide (Gruttadaro et al., 2007) states, much remains to be learned about the long-term safety and effectiveness of psychotropic medications for children. The authors noted that the younger the child, the less research is available. Thus, both practitioners and families need to approach decisions about the use of medication with great caution, with careful attention to the potential risks and benefits, and with consideration of the severity of the child's symptoms and their impact on functioning. One problem is that many psychotropic medications prescribed for young people with mental illness are not approved by the Food and Drug Administration (FDA) for use in children but are routinely used off label, a common practice among family physicians and psychiatrists. This occurs largely because of the limited research conducted with young patients. Nevertheless, although much of the research has been conducted with adults, there is increasing evidence for the effectiveness of medication with children and adolescents (Marsh & Fristad, 2002).

Many resources are available that describe psychotropic medications prescribed for children, including the Web sites of pharmaceutical companies, which provide much consumer-friendly information, and the *Physicians' Desk Reference* (2008). The National Institute of Mental Health (NIMH, 2000) has developed a family guide, *Treatment of Children With Mental Disorders*, that offers a useful medication chart that includes stimulant, antidepressant, antianxiety, mood-stabilizing, and antipsychotic medications as well as information about brand names, generic names, and approved age. As we noted, however, the field is changing rapidly, and practitioners and families need to stay abreast of new psychopharmacological developments.

Professional Roles and Responsibilities

Families often have contact with several mental health professionals and may be confused about these individuals' roles and responsibilities. Depending on their training and experience, professionals may undertake diagnostic evaluations, offer treatment recommendations, provide psychotherapy, prescribe and monitor medication, or fulfill other responsibilities. The roles of professionals vary to some extent across states, which establish standards for licensing and clinical practice for each profession. For example, although prescriptive authority is often restricted to psychiatrists and other medical practitioners, psychologists are now able to prescribe medication in some states. Similarly, although all states license psychiatrists, psychologists, and social workers, there is some variability in the licensing of other professionals, which may affect insurance reimbursement. Clinicians should be familiar with any restrictions in licensing and practice in their state.

Other professionals may also play an important role in diagnosis and treatment. For example, pediatricians can evaluate whether medical problems may be causing or contributing to the mental health problems. As Morey and Mueser (2007) noted in their book, *The Family Intervention Guide to Mental Illness*, medical problems that can cause psychological symptoms include thyroid imbalance, brain trauma due to head injury, exposure to toxic chemicals, hormonal shifts, effects of surgery or illness, and fluctuation in blood sugar levels due to diabetes or hypoglycemia. Similarly, school psychologists and guidance personnel play essential roles in developing and implementing Individualized Education Programs (or Plans) (IEPs), as discussed in Chapters 4 and 5.

In the case of child or adolescent mental illness, however, families will have most frequent contact with mental health professionals and can benefit from a brief overview of these different professionals:

- Child and adolescent psychiatrists, who have a medical degree (MD) and additional training in psychiatry, are qualified to undertake comprehensive psychiatric evaluations, treat psychiatric disorders, and prescribe and monitor medications.
- Clinical psychologists, who have a doctorate in psychology (PhD or PsyD), are qualified to conduct comprehensive psychological evaluations, to diagnose mental illness, and to offer individual, family, and group therapy.
- Clinical social workers, who have a master's degree (MSW), may provide various services, such as assessment and treatment of mental illness, case management, and hospital discharge planning.
- Licensed professional counselors (LPCs), who have a master's degree in psychology, counseling, or a related field, may provide various services, such as assessment and treatment of mental illness, including individual, family, and group counseling.
- Marriage and family therapists, who have a master's degree (MFT), may provide various services, such as assessment and treatment of mental illness, including individual, family, and group counseling.
- Psychiatric/mental health nurses, who have various degrees, may provide a range of psychiatric and medical services, including assessment and treatment of mental illness, case management, and in some states, prescription and monitoring of medication.

In addition, families may have contact with other professionals, such as certified alcohol and drug abuse counselors.

Helping Families Cope

Several resources are designed to help families understand the mental health system. These include the *Family Guide to Systems of Care for*

Children With Mental Health Needs, which is available from SAMHSA (2005). The guide is designed to help families learn what they need to know, which questions to ask, what they can expect, and what they can do. A useful glossary is included. We provide a brief overview of the material in the guide, which can facilitate discussions between clinicians and families.

Obtaining Services

Reflecting current models of family-driven or family-centered care, the guide (SAMHSA, 2005) emphasizes that families are the experts when it comes to their child, that they will decide which services and supports their child and family will receive, and that there is much they can do to meet their child's needs. The guide suggests that families begin a file that includes information about their child. The file should include reports of tests and evaluations; service plans and information about providers, programs, and services they are using; instructions from professionals who are working with their child and family; changes in their child's behavior; information about prescribed medication; notes from appointments and meetings; requests that families have made; and letters about meetings and services as well as the dates they were received.

Beginning with the initial referral or intake, the guide (SAMHSA, 2005) charts the process of obtaining services for the child and family. Families are informed that the initial visit may take place in a variety of settings, and that most programs and services have eligibility criteria. They are encouraged to learn which services and supports are available, how eligibility for services is determined, how much services cost, and what assistance is available to pay for them. Families also need to ask about the frequency and duration of services; what they should do get help during a crisis, especially at night or on a weekend when the office is closed; and how they can find respite care and other support to maintain their child at home. If they are told that their child and family are not eligible for services at that agency, they need to ask for a referral to another service or program.

When they attend their first meeting, families should bring their file of information, identification, and proof of medical insurance, a Medicaid card, or evidence of their need for financial assistance, such as a pay stub. They can write down their questions before they attend the meeting and write down the answers to their questions. They also need information about the agency's services, fees, payment options, procedures, and appeal process. The initial meeting is likely to include interviews with the child and family as well as the completion of paperwork, such as permission for the child to be tested, permission to obtain or release information, and agreement to accept and pay for services.

Following the initial session, the family will work with individual service providers and a service-planning team. The service plan should include goals, individualized services and supports as close to home as possible, and regular progress reports. The *service plan* is a written document that describes all the services and supports the child and family will receive. The plan usually includes information about the strengths, problems, and needs of the child and family; what the services and supports are designed to accomplish; and how and when progress will be assessed.

A service coordinator or case manager is often assigned, although families sometimes serve in that role. Families need to ask about the qualifications and experience of service providers and how the plan is expected to help their child and family. They can disagree with a provider and get a second opinion or change services or providers if they are dissatisfied but should be encouraged to consider the views and suggestions of providers, who are as interested in progress as families are. In their contacts with service providers, families need to let them know about the strengths of their child and family; their needs, wants, and expectations; and their preferences and priorities. As the service plan is implemented, families should monitor progress and let the service coordinator or case manager know if some part of the plan is not working as expected so the service planning team can make changes.

Understanding the Evaluation Process

As Wagner (2002a) pointed out, families may encounter some hurdles in the evaluation process, including inexact diagnostic methods that require both established guidelines and clinical judgment, an imperfect diagnostic system based on a certain number or configuration of symptoms rather than a holistic approach that captures all aspects of a child's functioning, and the frequent occurrence of multiple disorders. Especially in the case of serious mental illness, families may be given multiple diagnoses over time (Marsh, Koeske, & Schultz, 1993), which can be very confusing.

For example, the manifestations of major depression, bipolar disorder, and schizophrenia may each include psychotic symptoms, such as hallucinations and delusions. Depending on the presenting symptoms at the time of evaluation, the diagnosis might be any of those disorders or schizoaffective disorder. Over time, families may hear all of those diagnoses, with little understanding of the rationale. Even when the evaluation process proceeds smoothly, families may be reluctant to have their child "labeled" with a mental illness. Clinicians can assist families to anticipate and prepare for the evaluation process, to understand the results and recommendations, and to make an informed choice about treatment.

Making an Informed Decision Regarding Treatment

Following an evaluation, the treatment team may recommend multiple programs and services as well as both psychosocial and psychopharmacological interventions. Practitioners can assist families to become knowledgeable about each of the recommendations. When working with families, clinicians can assist them in making an informed decision about their use of services by discussing the available services, their potential risks and benefits, the risks of forgoing services, and possible alternatives. Families can also benefit from a discussion of research support for various services.

The NAMI guide (Gruttadaro et al., 2007) encourages families to talk with providers about treatment choices and EBP. Suggested questions include the following:

- Why are you recommending this treatment, and what are the alternative treatments, if any?
- What is the goal of the recommended treatment, and how will it help us achieve the outcomes we want?
- What are the risks and benefits associated with the recommended treatment?
- Is there research supporting the recommended treatment with families like ours?
- What training and experience do you have with the recommended treatment?
- How can our family best support the treatment?
- What changes can we expect to see, and how long will it be before we see these changes?
- How do we measure and monitor progress?
- What should we do if problems get worse or we do not see improvement?

Because families play an essential role in monitoring medication, its effectiveness in alleviating symptoms, and its side effects, they need to be knowledgeable about a prescribed medication. As Morey and Mueser (2007) discussed, medication is often effective in relieving the symptoms of mental illness, in preventing the recurrence of symptoms, and in improving the functioning of individuals. The right medication can reduce chronic anxiety and panic attacks, minimize or eliminate severe depression, level the bipolar cycles of manic highs and depressed lows, and eliminate or quiet the voices of schizophrenia. Once these symptoms are alleviated, patients can benefit more fully from psychosocial interventions.

Morey and Mueser (2007) pointed out that families usually appreciate an explanation of how medication works, noting that medications work by stimulating the production of chemicals that are under-produced in the brain or by preventing other chemicals from overproduction. These chemicals need to be in the right balance for the neurotransmitters to carry the signals of the brain accurately. They also observe that psychopharmacology is not an exact science, and that medication must be monitored continually. Finding the right medication for a particular individual and disorder often entails a trial-and-error process that may involve several medications. Moreover, it often takes time for a medication to work. An additional concern is the side effects that accompany medication. Depending on the child's symptoms, several medications may be combined. If a particular medication is not effective in alleviating symptoms or there are troubling side effects, other medications are available.

When medication is recommended, the NAMI guide (Gruttadaro et al., 2007) suggests that families ask certain questions, including the following:

- Are there psychosocial interventions that might be tried before medication is used or effectively used in combination with medication to lower the required dose?
- Does research support the use of the recommendation for children the age of my child and with similar needs?
- How does medication fit within the overall treatment plan?
- What changes in symptoms and behavior should we be looking for?
- What are the potential risks and benefits of the medication, possible side effects, and the other treatment options?
- How will we monitor progress, behavior changes, symptoms, and safety concerns?
- How will we know when it is time to stop medication and what steps need to be taken?

CHAPTER FOUR

Helping Families Understand the Educational System

Alex Michaels, a 16-year-old student, arrived with his parents at the emergency room of a psychiatric hospital that was 3 hours from their home. Meeting Dr. Stanley, the psychiatrist on duty that evening, Alex's parents explained that he had experienced increased behavior problems at school that led to many parent–teacher phone calls and conferences, afterschool detentions, and suspensions. Following his latest outburst, the principal of Alex's high school barred him from returning to school until he was "cured." After a comprehensive exam, Dr. Stanley diagnosed Alex with bipolar disorder and stated that Alex, like most people with mental illness, would need ongoing outpatient treatment: The "quick fix" demanded by the principal was unattainable. Alex and his parents returned to their home knowing the cause of Alex's outbursts but not how to proceed in working with the school to obtain assistance. Would sharing this information help Alex return to school? What rights did Alex have to obtain an education? What accommodations could the school make? What should they do if the school refused to provide the accommodations Alex needed?

Parents who are knowledgeable about both their child's mental ill-ness and the special education system possess three related advan-tages. First, they seem to experience a much easier time gaining full support from teachers and school districts because they are able to ar-ticulate their child's strengths and needs. Second, they are more com-fortable informing teachers about possible educational or behavioral difficulties and are able to do so without confrontational occurrences on either side. Third, due to this open and positive communication, they often acquire the needed services for their child in a timelier man-ner while having their own concerns addressed. In addition, when ser-vices are not being provided, their knowledge allows them to challenge the system to get what is needed for their child.

To assist mental health professionals and parents navigate the school maze more easily, this chapter focuses on the legal aspects of the edu-cation system, specifically in terms of special education. By under-standing the laws regulating decisions made by schools, families gain knowledge regarding the legal entitlements of children with mental ill-ness. Not only does this empower parents when working with the schools, but also it promotes a more equitable, cooperative, and open relationship that allows all interested parties to work together toward the joint goal of supporting and serving the child.

Special education is the term used to describe any individualized, planned changes in curriculum, instruction, or classroom placement. The term is descriptive, not derogatory. Many students need changes because they are different; education is not a one-size-fits-all venture. Currently, over 9% of school-aged children receive special education services under federal laws (U.S. Department of Education, 2005).

The foundation of special education rests mainly on two federal acts: the Individuals With Disabilities Education Act (IDEA) (U.S. De-partment of Education, 2006) and Section 504 of the Rehabilitation Act of 1973 (commonly referred to as Section 504 or just "504") (U.S. De-partment of Civil Rights, 2005). These two acts specify the guidelines for Individualized Education Programs (or Plans) (IEPs) and special education services. A third federal act, the Family Educational Rights and Privacy Act (FERPA), provides for confidentiality of all student records (U.S. Department of Education, 2007c). Examining these three acts provides a strong foundation for understanding special education and related services in schools.

Individuals With Disabilities Education Act

Prior to 1970, only 20% of American children with disabilities were educated; many states excluded students who had visual, hearing, emotional, or cognitive disabilities (U.S. Department of Education, 2007a). Then, in 1975, the U.S. Congress created the Education for All Handicapped Children Act (Public Law 94-142) to protect the educational rights of students with disabilities. In 1997, the name was changed to the Individuals With Disabilities Education Act (IDEA), reflecting a change in public perception about the definitions of the terms *handicapped* and *disability*.

Six major principles are provided by IDEA to guide actions of schools, specifically the right to (a) a free and appropriate public education (FAPE); (b) appropriate evaluations; (c) IEPs; (d) least restrictive environment (LRE); (e) parent and student participation; and (f) procedural safeguards. Knowledge of these principles provides a strong foundational understanding of the rights of students with disabilities.

According to the law, *free* means that education is provided at public expense; parents are not financially responsible for any special education or related services. This free clause does not apply to any incidental fees normally collected from nondisabled students. For example, if it is determined through appropriate assessment that a student needs a one-on-one aide, psychological counseling, and special books to meet the educational expectations set for the student, then the costs of these accommodations are paid for by the school district, not the parents. The parents would pay the fees for the graphic art class the student takes, as would parents of nondisabled students.

Under IDEA, federal funds are available to the school district to assist with the additional costs related to special education. In 2006, however, federal funds covered only 17.7% of the estimated costs (New America Foundation, 2007). Because school districts must pay for the majority of special education services, conflicts may arise when additional services are cost prohibitive, such as services from speech pathologists, registered nurses, or behavioral strategists. Although most districts do find the funds to provide the necessary services, some districts are resistant. They may attempt to offer no services or to limit services to save money. Namely, what is "best" for students and what are "appropriate services" often differ. In these cases, parents, sometimes with the assistance of legal experts, need to advocate on behalf of their child.

Appropriate Education

According to IDEA, education needs to be individualized when a student has a disability, and what is appropriate differs for each student. Students need to be evaluated by qualified personnel within the school to determine what is needed or appropriate. For example, one student with an anxiety disorder might need extra time to take tests or to take tests in a resource room; another student with the same disorder might need counseling in an emotional support class during the day. Even if the diagnostic label is the same, the students' needs might not be; therefore, IDEA mandates that for the education to be considered appropriate, it must correspond with the students' needs.

To ensure that the needs of students are met appropriately, educators nationwide are employing response to intervention (RtI) within classrooms. Specifically, teachers using RtI continually assess students' achievement and intervene using evidence-based methods to promote achievement and reduce behavior problems (Johnson, Mellard, Fuchs, & McKnight, 2006). Students identified as needing intervention may not be students with disabilities but merely may be students who are not attaining expected grade-level achievements. By using RtI, students who simply do not have the skills will begin to achieve, and students with disabilities will be more easily identified. Also, RtI helps address the issue of disproportionality and overidentification of certain groups of students based on race and ethnicity.

Least Restrictive Environment

The premise of IDEA is that no child should be excluded from school or society; LRE takes this premise and clarifies its implementation in the classroom. Specifically, LRE means that students with disabilities are to be educated with their nondisabled peers as long as the desired educational outcomes are possible within the regular classroom; accommodations and services may be used to make that education possible. For example, a student diagnosed with schizophrenia might talk aloud to unseen entities in class. Under LRE, the student would not be sent to a separate room for all instruction due to these outbursts as such a placement would violate LRE. Instead, the teacher might ignore the actions with no reprimand, redirect the student, or instruct other students to ignore the talking.

Implementing LRE sends a powerful message to students both with and without disabilities: All students are equal and worthwhile. No one is segregated or sent a message of inferiority, as occurred prior to IDEA. Receiving instruction in a regular classroom allows students with disabilities to make friends with a wide array of students, to observe what is normal and acceptable behavior, and to view themselves in a more positive light. For example, if a student with depression were in a class filled only with similar students, behaviors such as social withdrawal, irritability, or self-injury might become the norm; the actions of nondepressed students might seem odd. In-class accommodations and RtI allow students with disabilities to learn with their same-age peers whenever beneficial.

According to IDEA, however, students can be educated away from their nondisabled peers "when the nature or severity of the disability of a child is such that education in regular classes with the use of supplementary aids and services cannot be achieved satisfactorily" [U.S. Department of Education, 2006, Sec. 612 (a)(5)(A)]. For example, if a student's IEP states that the student will receive counseling in school twice per week, the student can be away from nondisabled peers during that time. Likewise, if a student has experienced psychotic symptoms and cannot be in school, that child might be homeschooled until the psychosis is under control and the student can return.

Public

Public refers to the right of students to an education, no matter how severe their disability. This policy, also known as the "zero-reject" policy, reverses earlier patterns when children with disabilities were offered public education only if they could fit into a regular education classroom. For students with disabilities to be included in public schools, special accommodations are available. For instance, a student diagnosed with bipolar disorder might have an inability to concentrate or sit still in his or her seat. An educational plan would be designed to address these issues and to adapt the instruction, curriculum, or resources as needed. So, instead of being yelled at or earning detentions for the behavior, the student might receive preferential seating, additional reminders, or extra assistance.

One of the accommodations made under FAPE focuses on suspensions. According to IDEA, a student with an IEP cannot be suspended for more than 10 days if the behavior is related to the disability; this relationship can be determined during a manifestation hearing, often consisting of the people on the IEP team. If the behavior is related to the disability, the student cannot be suspended beyond 10 days. However, the IEP team typically revisits the IEP for appropriateness and often adds a functional behavior plan.

If it is determined that the behavior was not caused by the disability, then the student may be suspended for more than 10 days, similar to nondisabled peers, although special education services must continue throughout the manifestation hearing and the long-term suspension. This means that the district is responsible for either homeschooling or an out-of-district placement. If a student brings a weapon or illegal drugs to school, the district can suspend the student for up to 45 calendar days, but must continue to provide access to the general curriculum. In one case, a student brought a box cutter to school for the purpose of cutting herself; she was suspended for 45 days for having a weapon even though her psychiatrist vouched that the knife was not being brought to school as a weapon.

Individualized Education Plans

The IEPs specify the educational plans for students with disabilities. Each contains information mandated by IDEA, including the student's current performance, annual goals, special education and related services, participation with nondisabled students, participation in statewide tests, dates and places, transition services and age of majority (if needed), and measures of progress.

The student's current levels of academic achievement and functional performance, including how the child's disability affects involvement and progress in the general curriculum, are determined by results of evaluations by both in-school personnel and out-of-school personnel (when applicable). For example, based on the diagnosis of a psychiatrist, the observations of teachers and parents, and the insights of the school psychologist, the following might be part of what is written to describe the achievement level of a student diagnosed with bipolar disorder (Papolos & Papolos, 2006):

> Joseph is a likable boy who was diagnosed with bipolar disorder three years ago. . . . His moods may veer from feeling hopeless and negative and depressed . . . to times in which he will appear energized, grandiose, and superior to some of his classmates. . . . Joseph has been quite stable on medication, but side effects such

as fatigue and cognitive dulling can impact his availability and ability to learn. (p. 306)

This description, which might include additional information about his time on task, organization abilities, interpersonal skills, or other pertinent information, frames Joseph's needs and thus his IEP.

Annual goals set realistic, measurable objectives for the year in terms of the student's academic, social, and behavioral progress. The IEP must state "how the child's progress will be measured and how parents will be informed of that progress" (U.S. Department of Education, 2007b, par. 34). Although short-term objectives or "benchmarks" may be included as part of the annual goals, they are no longer mandated by IDEA. Because benchmarks force educators to assess students' progress toward their annual goals with specific dates, it is beneficial to include them.

For example, if the present level of achievement for Joseph, the student just mentioned, includes a maximum of 15 minutes on task, then one of the annual goals might be that he would stay on task independently for 30 minutes by the end of the year (Papolos & Papolos, 2006). The short-term objectives supporting this goal might include gradually lengthening his time on task, first with teacher cues and then without. By structuring annual goals in terms of short-term objectives, teachers and parents can assess how well the student is progressing.

Behavior Plan

A behavior plan, which is focused on decreasing negative behaviors or on increasing positive ones, should be included within these annual goals. The annual goals allow everyone, including parents, the student, teachers, and other school personnel, to understand what the student is expected to be doing by the year's end and the steps that will be taken to reach these goals.

According to IDEA, parents of children with disabilities are required to be informed of progress at least as often as parents of nondisabled children, but IDEA does not specify how the parents will be informed (Petska, 2006); the IEP must state how the parents will be informed. For example, in some school districts, a grade report is sent home one time per quarter, merely reporting grades. Depending on the student and the disability, these sparse reports may not provide sufficient information frequently enough to determine a student's progress. If a parent desires progress reports more often or in a different format (e.g., a narrative format), this needs to be written in the IEP to force compliance. This request should be realistic regarding the frequency and depth of reports.

Services

The IEP must also list the special education and related services to be provided. This includes modifications to the program, special placement (e.g., an emotional support room), and supplementary aids and services (e.g., an aide). For example, modifications might include extra time on tests, breaking assignments into manageable parts, providing an aide (either one on one or placed in the classroom), or instruction provided at home if the disorder prevents the student from attending school (Papolos & Papolos, 2006.) The IEP specifies when the services are to begin, how often they will occur (e.g., once a week, daily), where they will be provided (e.g., within the regular classroom), and what the duration will be.

The IEP must explain if and when the student will not participate with nondisabled students in regular classes or other school activities. For example, some students with mental illness attend an emotional support classroom each day for one class period and receive extra assistance or counseling at that time. This would be considered time "away" from nondisabled students. Similarly, some students with mental illness do not do well with changes in the daily routine or with too much environmental stimulation. In these cases, the IEP might state that the student could go to the office or to an emotional support classroom instead of a pep rally-style assembly. Similarly, the IEP must state whether the student will take the statewide or schoolwide standardized achievement tests like nondisabled students; adaptations such as extended time, changes in physical location, or additional breaks might be provided. Due to the No Child Left Behind Act, avoiding these standardized exams is difficult.

The IEP Team

To create the IEP, an IEP team is formed consisting of not less than one regular education teacher, not less than one special education teacher, a representative of the school district (e.g., a principal), and a parent. Usually, all of the student's teachers are included in the meeting; however, if the modifications or discussion do not relate to an IEP team member's area *and* if the parents and school representative agree, that team member may be excused from the meeting. Some experts contend that excusing team members removes important voices from the discussion; others assert that the meetings merely waste those team members' time. During the initial meeting, team members share their views and suggest ideas for the IEP.

If team members recognize a need for changes during the course of the year, a full IEP team meeting may be called or, under amendments made in 2004, a phone conference with parents may be utilized. Again, some experts perceive a phone call as a more efficient means of serving the child's immediate needs, but others contend that the lack of face-to-face time eliminates the full consideration that is promoted by direct discussions. This decision is ultimately up to the parents.

If students are capable of making mature decisions, including them at the IEP meeting is beneficial: Making decisions for students without their consent may lead to resentment, resistance, or retaliation that can defeat the system. For example, if a student feels embarrassed or singled out by having to take tests in a separate room, he or she might quietly refuse or loudly demonstrate against this; in either case, the IEP would not be followed.

Transitions and Transfers

When an IEP is written for a student who is 16 (or younger, if deemed appropriate by the IEP team), a transition plan needs to go into effect. The transition plan focuses on postsecondary goals related to "training, education, employment, and, where appropriate, independent living skills" and on what the student will need to reach those goals (U.S. Department of Education, 2006, par. 4). To design these goals, the IEP team assesses the student's skills in various areas (e.g., cognitive, emotional, independent living) and may set up a trial experience. For example, if a student with an anxiety disorder wants to attend college after graduating from high school, an assessment might include taking a course at a local university while still in high school. The student and the IEP team could assess the student's comfort level and academic success and then use these data to determine specific postsecondary goals (e.g., to attend college or not, to attend college close to home, or to attend a small college versus a large university).

Although putting a realistic plan into action is important, parents and schools need to remember that the track one begins on in high school often determines a student's options. For example, if a student does not decide that college is a viable option until the end of his 10th-grade year, courses required for postsecondary education may be skipped, such as higher-level math, a foreign language, or college prep English. Therefore, it is highly recommended that the IEP team begin discussing the transition plan by the end of eighth grade when possible. In addition, the IEP must include a statement that "the student has been told of any rights that will transfer to him or her at the age of majority" (U.S. Department of Education, 2007a, para. 31).

The process to be followed when a student with an IEP transfers to a new school was clarified by revisions made to IDEA in 2004 (U.S. Department of Education, 2006). According to the revisions, the new school must basically follow the IEP that arrives with the student, continuing to provide comparable services until a new IEP is designed, approved, and implemented. If the IEP from the prior school is deemed acceptable, the new school still needs to approve it via an IEP meeting (Families and Advocates Partnership for Education, 2004).

Parent and Student Participation

According to IDEA, the IEP needs to be developed with the participation of parents and, when appropriate, students. No evaluation or testing can be undertaken by the school without informed consent by the parents. Within a short time of the referral (differing from state to state, but generally about 2 weeks), the school must send parents either a request for consent or a notice that the school has determined that no additional assessments are needed (Petska, 2006). Schools must complete their initial evaluation within 60 days of receiving consent; thus, the earlier the parents agree, the earlier in the school year the child can receive services. Likewise, the earlier in the year a parent requests an evaluation, the earlier the child may receive services. Parental consent is also necessary to implement the services initially and to reevaluate the student. If parents refuse to give consent, the school cannot provide an IEP.

Parents are given copies of the procedural safeguards, which explain their right to contest the outcomes of the evaluation; the instruction, curriculum, or placement according to the IEP; and the services provided. These safeguards are written in great detail in IDEA. Obviously, the best place to bring up these grievances is at the initial IEP meeting when the outcomes of the evaluation are discussed and the IEP is designed. However, some parents sign the IEP despite feeling that there is too much information to digest instantly or that school personnel are ganging up on them in an unfair situation. In these cases, parents should be encouraged to ask for a copy of the IEP to take home to examine. They can later choose to sign or amend the IEP. Also, for parents who feel apprehensive about the IEP meeting, special education advocates are often available; some offer free services, although some charge high rates. It is suggested that parents choose an advocate or attorney with training and expertise in special education as well as someone who understands their child and their concerns.

Sometimes, what a parent wants or feels the child needs conflicts with what the school views as beneficial or necessary. In these cases, mediation may be needed. According to the procedural safeguards, a trained impartial mediator facilitates the discussion between the parents and the school. A signed agreement can be created during mediation, allowing both parties to consensually create a working plan. Each party pays for their own lawyers, if applicable (Yell, 2006). If no agreement is reached through mediation, a due process hearing occurs in which an impartial hearing officer provided by the school district acts as a judge to resolve the issue (Yell, 2006). This decision can be appealed to the federal district court and on from there. During mediation and hearings, the child's services continue as they are due to a "stay put" clause in IDEA.

Section 504

There are 13 categories of disabilities identified by IDEA, and IDEA specifies that the disability must negatively affect a student's academic performance in a significant way, which limits the number of students with disabilities who qualify for special education under IDEA. For example, if a student has an anxiety disorder, that student would only qualify for an IEP if he or she showed a significant limitation in social and emotional areas to a degree that his or her learning is negatively impacted. Hence, if the disability is not considered severe enough, the student might not qualify under IDEA. However, the student with a disability might qualify to receive accommodations at school under Section 504 of the Rehabilitation Act. To qualify under Section 504, individuals with disabilities are defined as by the U.S. Department of Civil Rights (2005) as

persons with a physical or mental impairment which substantially limits one or more major life activities . . . [or] who have a history of, or who are regarded as having, a physical or mental impairment that substantially limits one or more major life activities. . . . Some examples of impairments which may substantially limit major life activities, even with the help of medication or aids/devices, are: AIDS, alcoholism, blindness or visual impairment, cancer, deafness or hearing impairment, diabetes, drug addiction, heart disease, and mental illness. (par. 3)

This means that all students covered under IDEA are also covered by Section 504; however, the reverse is not true (see Figure 4.1).

In the context of serving students with mental illness, two points of the law are worth highlighting. First, people diagnosed with a mental illness automatically qualify for the protections granted by Section 504.

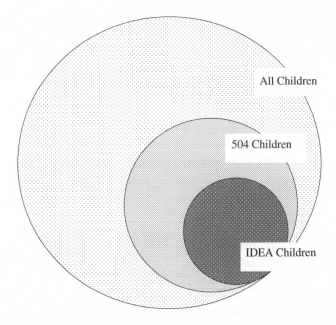

Figure 4.1. Relationship of Section 504 and IDEA children. From "Relationship of Section 504 and IDEA Children," by S. J. Rosenfeld dba Edlaw (2008). Used with permission of the author.

This means that whether their disability affects their educational progress or not, students have the right to claim special education services if needed. According to Section 504, these services could "consist of education in regular classrooms, education in regular classes with supplementary services, and/or special education and related services" (U.S. Department of Civil Rights, 2005, par. 14). Second, these rights are not affected by whether the student is taking medication or has other support services. Thus, if a child with an anxiety disorder takes medication and outwardly appears to be "doing fine" at school, that child might still receive services in school, such as counseling, changes in test locations, or accommodations during standardized tests.

Processes and Services

Although students can receive services under the auspices of IDEA or Section 504, the processes and services are not identical in terms of evaluation, planning and implementation, parental involvement, and length of applicability. Therefore, it is important to understand the differences between them.

The Department of Education governs IDEA, whereas the Office of Civil Rights administers Section 504. The former provides funds to assist with additional costs related to special education; uses multidisciplinary, school-based evaluations to determine needs; and is implemented by special education professionals. In contrast, Section 504 has no funding; and schools must pay for any accommodations they provide. Although Section 504 states that supplementary services, special education, and alternative placements must be provided if needed, students who qualify only under Section 504 usually have their accommodations made solely by the regular classroom teacher. For Section 504, knowledgeable individuals, such as mental health professionals, are able to determine whether a student qualifies. Thus, if a student diagnosed with bipolar disorder has major outbursts that affect his or her ability to learn, the student may be covered under IDEA; if that student succeeds without accommodations comparably with peers, he or she might qualify only under Section 504.

The 504 "Plan"

Under Section 504, a "plan" is necessary but not an IEP. Unlike an IEP, which has its content specified by federal law, a plan under Section 504 can take many forms. Parents need to be informed about the plan and any changes made to it, but their consent is not required. As with the IEP, related services and accommodations on standardized testing must be listed. However, under Section 504, no specific annual goals or progress reports are required.

The concept of FAPE applies to 504 students, but in a different way than their IDEA counterparts. Students whose disabilities are considered severe enough that they need a *special* education, with changes made to the education curriculum, instruction, or assessments, are supported by IDEA. Section 504 provides *access* to education. Although the plan can include changes in curriculum, instruction, or assessment, these changes are designed to allow the 504 student to do the same work that a nondisabled student is doing.

Section 504 does not offer the same protection as IDEA for students regarding suspensions: If a student's behavior is not directly related to the disability identified in the 504 plan, the student can be suspended like any other student for any amount of time; no continuation of educational goals is mandated, and no 45-day rule applies. As with IDEA, a manifestation hearing is held to determine whether the suspension is allowed. If disabled students possess illegal drugs, alcohol, or weapons at school, they face the same disciplinary action as nondisabled students (Richards, 1999). Under Section 504, parents have a legal right to appeal that is similar to IDEA if they believe that the identification, evaluation, placement, or services received by their child are not appropriate. However, the "stay put" clause does not apply under Section 504.

Under IDEA, the needs of students with special needs are addressed until the students are 21 years of age (or graduate from high school, whichever comes first). Section 504 covers the lifespan of any person with disabilities, with the aim of removing barriers that would impede full participation in education as well as employment, transportation, and other essential activities. This means that when a student with a disability graduates from high school, future support is provided only under Section 504. If the student goes on to postsecondary education, the only accommodations are those that provide "appropriate academic adjustments and auxiliary aids and services that are necessary to afford an individual with a disability an equal opportunity to participate in a school's program" (U.S. Department of Health and Human Services, 2008, par. 7). Unlike the accommodations under IDEA, the accommodations at the postsecondary level cannot result in "fundamental alterations," such as adapting a test, changing the grading scale for a particular student, or reducing the amount of work a student needs to do.

Family Educational Rights and Privacy Act

According to the FERPA, schools may not share any specific information about a child's educational experiences (e.g., grades, IEP, or material that may identify the student) without written consent of the parent or eligible student (students 18 years or older). Exceptions include disclosing records to other school officials with legitimate educational interest, to a different school if the student is transferring, to specified officials for audit or evaluation purposes, to appropriate parties in connection with financial aid to a student, to officials in cases of health and safety emergencies, and to state or local officials within the juvenile justice system per state law (U.S. Department of Education, 2007c).

Educational records include written documents, computer files, photographs, and video/audio tapes that contain information directly related to a student or can identify the student individually. Examples include a teacher's note placed in a student's file, a psychiatrist's evaluation of a student, and a student's IEP. Personal notes used only by the person who made them are not considered educational records *unless* they are shared with another person, at which point they become educational records. Directory information (e.g., name, address, phone number, dates of attendance) may be disclosed without consent, but schools must inform parents about the directory and provide adequate time for parents to opt out of being included.

Under FERPA, parents or eligible students have the right to examine educational records, to demand that schools correct inaccurate or misleading records, and to obtain a formal hearing if the school decides not to correct the records. Schools must provide copies of all records if failing to do so would prevent parents from inspecting the records fully; however, schools are permitted to charge a fee for copies made. This right to examine educational records includes the right to inspect and receive explanations about assessments, grades, in-file notes, and so on; these explanations must be given within 45 days of a request.

CHAPTER FIVE

Helping Families Cope With the Educational System

Over the past year, 15-year-old Amber Mellner's behavior and grades had declined quickly. After many meetings with her teachers, the school counselor, and the principal, Amber's mother took her to a psychiatrist, who diagnosed her with early-onset schizophrenia. Mrs. Mellner informed the principal of this diagnosis, sending a copy of a letter from the psychiatrist. A meeting was set up to design an Individualized Education Plan (IEP) for Amber; Mrs. Mellner was asked to bring in copies of all relevant documents. The principal also invited Amber to the meeting but said her participation was optional. Mrs. Mellner preferred that her daughter not attend. When she arrived at the meeting, 10 people were sitting around the large conference table, waiting for her. They introduced themselves in a quick manner, and Mrs. Mellner recognized the principal, the school counselor, and the names of four of Amber's teachers; she did not catch the names or roles of the others at the table. The meeting began with each teacher sharing in full detail the behavioral and academic problems they had experienced with Amber. Although the behaviors reported were not new to Mrs. Mellner, hearing them stated in such detail and in front of so many people felt embarrassing and demeaning. It was as if Amber was their problem rather than that Amber had problems. When two of the participants began making suggestions for accommodations in school, Mrs. Mellner felt she had no voice in the proceedings: She was not an educator and believed she had no valid say in the educational choices made for her daughter. She was unfamiliar with some of the terms used but recognized that everyone else was familiar with them. The single time she ventured to speak up, someone stated, "No, that won't work." She did not dare offer more suggestions. At the end of the meeting, Mrs. Mellner was given a stack of papers, asked to sign a number of forms, and thanked for coming to the meeting. She wanted to read through the papers before signing but felt railroaded by the group to sign them immediately. She left feeling as if she had been through a battle, defeated in her attempts to help her daughter in the school. The school had provided a copy of an IEP draft for her, but she could not decipher what the various parts meant. She was unable to explain to her daughter what changes would occur at school. Although she fervently hoped that the school would provide her daughter with everything necessary, Mrs. Mellner was worried. Was keeping her daughter in this school the best choice? What rights and responsibilities did she have in these decision-making meetings? What knowledge did she need prior to entering this meeting? What could she have done differently?

As participants in many parent meetings for students with special needs, we have seen parents who traverse the spectrum of knowledge about special education and mental illness. Some, like Mrs. Mellner, arrive with no knowledge about what to expect, sit silently listening as a "judgment" is made about their child, and leave in tears, feeling that they are not able to be active participants in their child's educational life due to their lack of knowledge. Others arrive with an entourage of support, mounds of papers, and a list of demands beyond what the school can offer, an approach that precludes any type of meaningful dialogue needed to support the student. Obviously, neither end of this spectrum is conducive to creating an optimal program for a student. Instead, all parties need to come to the table as equal, informed participants able to disagree respectfully and openly ask questions to achieve the shared goal of providing appropriate accommodations for the student.

To work effectively with school personnel, parents need to understand the role of the school in the life of the student, who the key players will be in the student's school life, and how those players can come together with the family to create a system of support for the student, family, and teachers. This collaborative approach increases the likelihood that the student will receive the educational services needed to fulfill his or her potential.

For most students, school offers a chance to learn academic subjects, experience important social opportunities, and become involved in extracurricular activities. For students with mental illness, the following statement remains true (Canadian Mental Health Association, 2004):

> High school is a key setting for providing support for young people who are struggling with mental health problems. High school staff have an important role to play in ensuring that these students maintain their education, because it is within the high school environment that they will develop not only skills for learning, but also skills for positive peer relationships and skills necessary for emotional well-being. (Introduction, par. 4)

Therefore, the paramount goal is to enable students with mental illness to continue their education and to accomplish their goals. When possible, education should take place within the regular public school. Due to the complexity and severity of mental illness, however, this is not always possible. Sometimes hospitalization, behavioral issues, or the manifestations of the illness preclude placement in public school. Other placements are discussed in this chapter, but initially we look at the structure and composition of public schools.

School Personnel and Their Roles

As mentioned in Chapter 4, the experiences and knowledge of school personnel vary greatly: Some have extensive training and experience in working with students who have mental illness; others have none. Likewise, some personnel are very open, flexible, and willing to make accommodations and support students, but others add to the problems of students by increasing stress, remaining inflexible, and ignoring students' needs. Because every situation is different, we present the traditional roles of various personnel and offer suggestions for what each can do to support students with mental illness.

Classroom Teachers

In elementary school, children will usually have one classroom teacher who is responsible for all subjects. These teachers are generally good at noticing changes in behavior because they see the children all day, every day. Also, elementary children are known for tattling to the teacher whenever a peer does something wrong or odd. In secondary school (including junior high, middle school, and high school), teachers usually instruct in one discipline, and students may have more than eight teachers per day. Depending on the size of the class, the number of students, and other issues (including the rapport of teachers with students and their observations and insights), teachers may or may not recognize changes in behavior as quickly. Also, because the changes caused by mental illness are often subtle and may emerge over time, teachers may not notice the changes. Nonetheless, classroom teachers are often the first adult to recognize the characteristic changes in behavior, mood, attitude, and schoolwork.

When teachers are knowledgeable about mental illness, they ask parents whether these changes have been noticed at home. For example, a normally happy elementary child began crying every day when she went to school. She reported to the teacher, "I am so sad, and I just want to cry," but could not explain why. The teacher approached the parents, saying, "I'm worried about your daughter. She cries every day at school. Do you think she could be depressed?" In that particular case, the girl was crying due to a loss in her family that occurred 3 months prior. However, it was obvious that the teacher knew her students, observed their behavior, and understood that mental illness occurs in people of all ages. When ignorant about mental illness, teachers often call parents to report "problem" behaviors: sleeping in class, not paying attention, missing class often, being exceptionally disorganized, ignoring deadlines, or having serious emotional outbursts. They do not realize that these patterns could be part of a mental illness and may even blame the student or parent for the outward behaviors. Nonetheless, both well-trained and nontrained teachers are often the first to recognize these behaviors and to alert the parents, counselors, and school psychologist.

Classroom teachers are often responsible for implementing the accommodations within the classroom. Some do it well, some need to be trained in implementation, and some refuse to implement accommodations despite clear directives in the IEP. For example, a fifth-grade student with depression often failed to write her assignments correctly in the school-provided assignment book. According to her IEP, the general education teacher was to make sure the assignment was written correctly and, if it was not, to write it in the book for the student. The teacher refused to check it or write it. She felt that this was not part of her job description and, as she "wouldn't do it for all of the other children" in class, she would not do it just for this one girl: It would be "unfair" to the others. The student's psychiatrist worked with her parents and social worker to ensure that the teacher followed the directives.

Special Education Teachers

Special education teachers are trained to work with students who have special needs; specialization areas include emotional support, learning support, and physical support. These teachers are often responsible for writing, communicating, and overseeing the implementation of students' IEPs. In addition, depending on a student's needs, they may work directly with the student, either in the regular classroom or in a separate room (sometimes called a "resource room" or an "emotional support class," depending on the needs of the students).

Transition Specialists

Transition specialists work with high school students and their parents to plan the transition from school to work or to further training or education. The transition specialist may coordinate a job experience that not only allows the student to learn job-related skills, but also to develop social skills and life skills. For example, a student might work as an assistant in a billing department. In addition to learning to use the computer, the student would also learn time management, organization, promptness, and more.

School Counselors

Depending on the school and the ratio of students to counselor, the counselor's job at a school may include any or all of the following: advising, motivating, and assessing students; teaching social skills and behavior modification; providing grief counseling; offering personal counseling; and coordinating information for teachers so that students obtain the support they need. School counselors often have expertise regarding mental illness and are usually strong advocates for all students. These two qualities make them a good first choice for parents who want to discuss their child's needs with a school employee.

School Psychologists

School psychologists evaluate students for cognitive, academic, social, emotional, and behavioral competencies. Based on observations as well as formal and informal evaluations (such as measures of intelligence and academic achievement), they develop "psych reports" for each child evaluated. As with the school counselor, the amount of time a school psychologist has to counsel students depends on the student-to-psychologist ratio and school circumstances. In some schools, a clinical psychologist is hired by the school for the sole purpose of providing counseling and support to students; however, due to the expense involved, this does not happen as often as is needed.

Social Workers

Social workers, who may be employees of the school or of a mental health agency, act as liaisons among home, school, and mental health agencies. They often work with families to get a full picture of a student's life and are thereby able to create better environments to help students succeed. With this additional insight, they may help determine which services are needed at home or after school for a child with a mental illness; they can also recommend support services for families. During meetings like the one described in the opening vignette, social workers may present information sent from a psychiatrist or other non-school-based mental health provider.

Nurses

Some schools have nurses who call parents when children are sick, administer first aid, and dispense medicine. However, nearly 75% of medication provided in school is administered by unlicensed personnel (McCarthy, Kelly, & Reed, 2000). According to the nurses who participated in this survey, top problems included giving an overdose or double dose of medicine, giving the wrong medicine, and giving medicine without authorization. Because state laws differ regarding the dispensation of medication in schools and each school sets its own guidelines, it is imperative for parents to find out who is giving medicine to their child. Further, students should know what their medication looks like, how much they should be taking, and how often they should be taking it.

An additional problem arises when students accept the medicine from the nurse or other personnel but do not actually swallow it. Sometimes, it is thrown away; other times, it is sold to other students, which obviously causes additional problems. Either way, if a student's behavior seems erratic and "not responsive" to medication taken in school, the school needs to be notified so that they can ensure proper administration of medicine.

Paraprofessionals

Paraprofessionals, often referred to as aides, are noncertified assistants employed by the school. Depending on the student's needs, aides can offer one-to-one assistance in class or provide help in organizing or completing assignments. Although it may make parents feel better to know that their child has a one-to-one aide, paraprofessionals are not trained as teachers or psychologists. In some cases, they are exceptional mentors who are patient and insightful as well as able to connect with the student, to provide security, and to increase the likelihood of success. In other cases, paraprofessionals may offer nothing more than adult supervision at best and a physical reminder of the student's mental illness at worst. If the student is able to obtain the assistance of a trained professional, such as a teacher or a psychologist, instead of a paraprofessional, parents should welcome the opportunity. If only a paraprofessional can be obtained, it is essential that the parent, teacher, and social worker communicate their expectations regarding the paraprofessional clearly.

Decision Making

School personnel are responsible for making day-to-day decisions about how to support students best in their educational pursuits. For students with mental disorders, these decisions are framed by IEPs, which are ideally developed jointly by school personnel, parents, and mental health professionals.

Multidisciplinary Team Meetings

The 10-person meeting described in the opening vignette of this chapter, referred to as a *multidisciplinary team* (MDT) meeting, is a realistic depiction of the MDT meeting, especially at the junior high, middle school, and high school levels. Although parents often make informal decisions in one-on-one conversations with teachers or counselors, official decisions that are written into a student's IEP occur during an MDT meeting. A school may request a MDT meeting if there are concerns about a possible disability. A parent can also request a MDT meeting to inform the broad base of educators about a child's mental illness and provide additional information. This is often helpful because, although IEPs list the necessary accommodations, they do not provide background or narrative about the individual student.

According to the Individuals With Disabilities Education Act (IDEA), certain school personnel must attend the MDT meeting, including a representative of the school district (usually a building administrator, such as the principal); at least one classroom teacher; at least one special education teacher; and a parent or guardian. However, depending on the school, the age of the student (e.g., high school versus elementary), and the severity of disorder, other personnel may be invited to the MDT meeting, including teachers from a variety of disciplines, a school psychologist, a school counselor, an emotional support teacher (if the school has one), a transition specialist, and a social worker. Depending on age, maturity, and emotional stability, the student may also be invited to the meeting.

This type of meeting usually occurs for one of two reasons: to begin the evaluation process or to develop an IEP based on that evaluation. The first case occurs when the core teachers find common obstacles in advancing a student's learning and believe that a disability may be the cause. At meetings scheduled for this reason, school personnel usually present documentation, such as poorly done assignments, darkly written narratives, or frequently cited behavioral problems. They will then request permission to evaluate the student for a disability. After evaluating the student, school personnel may request the second type of MDT to develop an IEP for the student. Although a psychiatrist's report will suffice as an evaluation, it is important to keep in mind that the educational diagnosis and the medical diagnosis may not match. Medical diagnoses are based on terminology found in the text revision of the *Diagnostic and Statistical Manual of Mental Disorders, Fourth Edition* (*DSM-IV-TR;* American Psychiatric Association, 2000), whereas educational diagnoses follow the terminology found in IDEA. A student with bipolar disorder might be labeled as having an "emotional disturbance" in the school, but that term is not used in the medical community.

In both types of meetings, parents ignorant of the process often feel outnumbered, overwhelmed, and railroaded into accepting whatever the school offers. To prevent this from happening, parents need to ask questions prior to the meeting, such as who will be present, what the specific purpose of the meeting is, and what (if anything) they should bring to the meeting. Also, when possible, parents should consider what would help their child and prepare a list of possible accommodations; if the student is able to contribute to this list, it adds viability and strength to the requests.

As in the vignette that introduced this chapter, parents sometimes feel ill-equipped during MDT meetings. Information is often shared quickly and in "educational-ese" with terms like *IEP, GAD* (generalized anxiety disorder), or *ADHD* (attention deficit/hyperactivity disorder) used casually and without additional explanation. Therefore, parents need to be coached to take detailed notes, to ask questions when they are confused, to summarize for clarification (e.g., "So what I'm understanding is . . ."), and, when needed, to request time after a meeting to digest information prior to making a decision. Although these might seem like easy tasks, they are often challenging for parents, especially those who are struggling to absorb the fact that their child may have a mental disorder.

Parent Advocates

Parents may opt to bring others with them to assist, such as an advocate. Advocates may be professionals with legal and educational expertise, or they may be friends who have gone through the MDT process with their own children. In either case, advocates often provide parents with increased understanding and a sense of security. Educational advocates are usually either lawyers or teachers with deep knowledge about laws governing disabilities and schools. It is strongly suggested that if a family wishes to use an advocate, they employ someone who specializes in cases of mental illness and establish what the advocate charges; some provide free services, and others charge an hourly fee.

If the student is in the care of a psychiatrist or clinical psychologist and has been assigned a social worker from the mental health care facility, the social worker may be invited. Working with the psychiatrist or psychologist, the social worker can explain to educators the nature of the mental illness and the effects (or side effects) of medication and suggest strategies to assist the child. It should be noted that although parents may ask the psychiatrist or psychologist to attend the MDT meeting, they seldom are able to attend; however, with the parent's permission, they may write a report that the social worker can share with the MDT.

Parental Roles

Whether attending with support or alone, parents should bring all relevant information to the MDT meeting. This includes information from a mental health provider regarding the diagnosis, severity, and duration of the mental illness; about any prior IEPs or changes in placement; and about any medication that the student is taking. All of this information may be used to inform the educators' understanding of the child's circumstances. For example, information about medication should include how often it is taken, whether it needs to be taken in school, and any possible side effects (e.g., nausea, sleepiness). When educators have a broader picture of the student's functioning at home and in school, they can more easily identify trends and patterns. As a result, all parties can better recognize the mental illness, monitor its course, and design services to meet the student's needs.

It is also the parents' responsibility to make sure that educators know the student's diagnosis, if one exists, and what that diagnosis entails. Without written permission, psychologists and psychiatrists are not allowed to share any information about their patients, even with the schools. As mentioned, educators are not always familiar with mental disorders and may see only the manifested behaviors. In a report on IDEA enforcement to the Senate Health, Education, Labor, and Pensions Committee Hearing, the American Academy of Child & Adolescent Psychiatry (AACAP, 2002) stated:

> The AACAP is particularly concerned about children and adolescents with serious emotional disturbances who are receiving special education services. These students may display a variety of emotions that range from depression to disruptive behavior, and many children and adolescents with these disorders too often go undiagnosed and untreated. Those with depression are overlooked and the others are viewed as "trouble makers." The stigma linking mental illnesses to violent behavior makes certain diagnosed illnesses a red flag for removing a child from the classroom. Schools want to remove fear and violence but good intentions may result in denying an education to these students with diagnosed mental illnesses. (pp. 2–3)

Thus, a school might remove a student just because of a diagnosis that is not fully understood or attempt to eradicate a "problem behavior" without understanding the underlying cause. Either way, the school could inadvertently escalate the problems for both the student and the family.

To inform the school further, parents can assist educators by sharing specifics about the child as a person, providing a "whole-person" view, and offering examples of what works at home. Students who experience problems in school often experience similar problems at home. Therefore, when a parent shares that his child becomes enraged at home, not just at school, educators have a more holistic view of the child and can create more effective plans. Parents' suggestions and insights about how to redirect the student or to deflect inappropriate behavior are indispensable.

For example, a parent recommended that if her son began to appear anxious or agitated, school personnel might ask him, "Do you need to take 5?" This phrase helped the student recognize his own behavior. As a result, he was able to determine whether he was okay in the classroom, needed 5 minutes by himself to calm down, or should go the office for an extended period of time to compose himself. This phrase, used consistently at home and in school, allowed the student to decide for himself what was needed. Likewise, if parents know that certain behaviors or stimulants are antecedents to behavioral outbursts or other manifestations of the mental illness, educators need to know. Although sharing this information is often difficult for parents who might feel that they will be judged as "bad" parents, it is imperative for everyone—educators and parents alike—to recognize that schools and families must work as a team with all players on the same side so that the essential support will be available.

A Collaborative Process

The MDT meetings should be arranged to reflect the notion that everyone is there to help the child and not to make judgments about the parents, teachers, or child. Parents and educators all need to go into the MDT meetings recognizing that decisions about a student's educational plan may not be completed in one sitting. Parents may need to take time to digest information, read documents, consult mental health professionals, and think about how a plan will affect their child. There is no reason why parents cannot take information home and return it later; parents need to ask for this, and educators need to offer it. Further, an IEP cannot go into effect without the parent's signature; no additional school services can be provided without the IEP in place. (See Chapter 4 for a discussion about parents' right to challenge IEPs.)

When arranging the MDT meeting, educators should explain to parents how the meeting will run, who will be there, and what outcomes are desired; parents should ask for this information if it is not offered. When possible, parents should enter the meeting with ideas of what they want for their child, separating these ideas into three categories: what they think their child *needs*, what they *want* for their child, and what would be optimal, but not necessary. For example, a parent might say, "My child needs an education; I want it to be at a local school; and if it were in the regular classroom, that would be optimal." However, if the manifestation of the child's mental illness means that an education is only available through an alternative school, that option may be acceptable. Note that even when everyone comes to the table with the desire to advance a child's education, disagreements may still occur due to different perspectives and experiences (information about appealing the student's services is found in Chapter 4).

Placements

One of the most significant decisions that parents and educators need to make for students with mental illness is whether they will continue in the local school, have an alternative placement, or take time to focus on treatment and recovery (Canadian Mental Health Association, 2004). For some students, this last choice is preferable; they cannot gain an education until they have the illness under control. For many students with mental illness, however, their day-to-day life continues with school as a main component. Indeed, attending a local school remains as one option and the first one to consider: Accommodations offer the necessary supports, and students continue to attend school as they always have. On the other hand, depending on the severity of the illness, the local school may not be an option. Alternative placements can offer parents, educators, and children viable, more appropriate options. Such placements include residential boarding schools, local alternative schools, and Web-based schools.

For some families, the behavioral manifestations of their child's illness are extreme, making home life difficult at best and dangerous at worst. In these cases, residential schools may offer an excellent alternative and provide the student and family with the necessary services. Alternative local schools often have faculty with specialized training, smaller class sizes, and more structure, allowing some students to succeed in ways that a local school cannot. The third alternative placement, online schooling, allows students to stay at home and to complete work at their own pace and without the stressors of attending school (e.g., other people or time constraints). As with other adaptations, educators and parents need to make this decision together, whenever possible, for the benefit of the student.

It is important to keep in mind that discussions about "best" placements and accommodations for students depend on whose perspective one is taking: the parents, the school, the mental health care provider, or the student. All of the key players need to have a clear understanding of the process, a willingness to share pertinent information about the child, a thorough understanding about how mental illness affects students, and a desire to help the student gain the best education possible. If these conditions are in place, then schools can become the ally that parents need in supporting their child's goals for education and the future.

CHAPTER SIX

Helping Families Cope
With Mental Illness

*I was afraid. I got so scared. I'm driving across the bridge
thinking I just want to run right off this bridge. Nobody's listening to me. I'm looking for help. They throw her out of school
and send her home with me. Mental Health won't take her in
because she hasn't tried to commit suicide again. She tried
three times. That's the only way they'll take her in. So they're
sending her home with me. What can I do? I'm driving off this
bridge. That's it, I'm done, I give up.*

These are words of a mother (we call her Marge) whose teenage
daughter has mental illness. By the time of her interview, Marge and
her daughter had been involved with the mental health system for
several years. In spite of her many contacts with professionals, however, this desperate mother said she received little assistance in coping
with her daughter's illness or with the system. Her frustration and
anguish were apparent during her interview: "I always feel like I'm
banging my head up against the wall. My daughter has ripped our
family apart, ripped us apart, given us so much grief." One of our goals

in writing this book was to increase the likelihood that mothers like Marge will receive the support they so urgently need.

As we discussed in Chapter 2, the challenges confronting these families are considerable. At the same time, reflecting the diversity of families in general, families of children with mental illness vary along a continuum of competence and differ in their strengths, limitations, needs, priorities, and goals. Some families are unusually effective in fulfilling their functions and coping with family disruptions and crises. Others may have difficulty fulfilling even their basic functions, perhaps because they are struggling with poverty, violence inside or outside the home, addictions, or debilitating health problems. Most families fall someplace in the middle of the continuum. Whatever their level of functioning, however, all families are likely to be unsettled by child or adolescent mental illness.

Initially, we discuss the general strategies that can assist families to cope with childhood mental illness across the diagnostic spectrum at home and in school. In other chapters, we suggest diagnostic-specific coping strategies. These general strategies have been adapted from many sources, including the publications mentioned in Chapters 7 through 10, as well as other resources, such as the Massachusetts General Hospital School Psychiatry Program and MADI Resource Center (http://www2.massgeneral.org/schoolpsychiatry/) and the Boston University Center for Psychiatric Rehabilitation (http://www.bu.edu/cpr/). Finally, we offer suggestions for enhancing family effectiveness and empowering families to cope not only with mental illness but also with other crises and transitions.

In working with families, clinicians need to highlight the importance of relevant coping skills in dealing with mental illness and to assess the strengths and limitations of particular families. Some families can benefit from a brief overview of necessary skills; others may be appropriate candidates for more intensive training, including homework assignments and role playing in sessions. Thus, the material in this chapter offers a general outline that can be modified to meet the needs of individual families and children.

Coping With Mental Illness at Home

There are many ways in which practitioners can help families cope with mental illness. First and foremost, however, as Fitzgibbons and Pedrick (2003) pointed out, all children need their parents to be their parents:

> All children need a loving relationship with their parents. They need parents who make decisions that are in the child's best interests, spend time with them regularly, treat them with respect and kindness, and communicate to them regularly that they are valued and loved unconditionally. (p. 135)

More specifically, clinicians can assist families to acquire the skills needed to cope effectively with their child's mental illness and with its consequences for their family. The following coping strategies are helpful across diagnostic categories.

Creating a Supportive Family Environment

All children benefit from a supportive family environment, but such an environment is especially important for those with mental illness. To foster a supportive environment, parents can:

- Create an environment that offers structure, stability, and consistency;
- Establish a sense of safety and authority, letting the child know that they will be there to offer assistance and support;
- Empathize with the child's feelings and concerns;
- Learn to express their concerns in a nonjudgmental way;
- Promote a family atmosphere characterized by open and direct communication, by mutual tolerance and respect, and by caring, commitment, and affection;
- Resolve differences in the family in a way that acknowledges the

perspectives of all family members and that results in a mutually acceptable solution;

- Avoid unnecessary criticism and conflict;
- Avoid making abrupt changes, which can cause upheaval in children who often have difficulty with transitions; and
- Talk as a family about what to say to people outside the family.

Taking Care of Themselves

Faced with the many challenges associated with child or adolescent mental illness, it is essential for parents to take care of themselves, striving to:

- Maintain a satisfactory balance in their lives that allows them to fulfill their commitments to others without neglecting themselves;
- Understand personal and family limits—perfection is not a reasonable goal;
- Place the mental illness in perspective as a single event in their lives;
- Maintain a healthy lifestyle that meets their needs for sleep, nutrition, exercise, and relaxation;
- Avoid a permanent crisis mode;
- Enlist the help of supportive family and friends;
- Seek out others who have shared their experience;
- Join a community or online support group;
- Nourish their talents and explore their interests;
- Do something special for themselves on a regular basis; and
- If appropriate, seek counseling for themselves, which is a wise investment under these circumstances.

Empowering Their Family

There is much that parents can do to empower themselves and their child. As Foa and Andrews (2006) observed, mental illness is widely misunderstood. Families of children and adolescents with mental illness are on the front line of the battle against stigma, which prevents people from getting the treatment they need and reinforces a sense of shame. Clinicians can encourage parents to:

- Fight the stigma associated with mental illness by countering misinformation with facts;
- Learn about their child's mental illness and its treatment so they can explain it to their child and to others inside and outside the family;
- Learn about local child-serving systems and community resources;
- Learn about the family experience of mental illness;
- Improve their coping skills, including their communication, problem-solving, stress management, and assertiveness skills (see section on enhancing family effectiveness);
- Play a constructive role in their child's treatment, supporting the treatment plan and enlisting their child's engagement in the plan; and
- Work with the child's therapist to implement home-based interventions that are consistent with the treatment plan.

Distinguishing Between the Child and the Disorder

Parents need to separate their child from the disorder. Depending on their child's diagnosis, families may have to cope with anxiety-related symptoms, disturbances of mood, potentially harmful or self-destructive behavior, socially inappropriate or disruptive behavior, or psychotic symptoms, such as hallucinations and delusions. It is helpful for parents to:

- Focus on the child behind the symptoms, who is not defined by the mental illness;
- Emphasize the child's other qualities, such as academic, artistic, or athletic ability;
- Recognize illness-related behaviors as symptoms of an illness, not a character flaw;
- Avoid responding to symptomatic behavior with frustration, criticism, or anger directed at the child;

- Remind the child that it is the illness—not the child—causing the symptoms; and
- Tell the child repeatedly that together they will fight the illness.

Adapting Their Parenting Style

In educating parents about the concept of goodness of fit, practitioners can point out that different parenting styles work with many children, although some children with particular problems function best with certain approaches to parenting. Just as parents need to adapt their role to accommodate a child with serious medical problems, parents of children with mental illness also may need to adapt their style and behavior. Some parents may already be parenting effectively; others may benefit from parent training designed to help them make changes that can assist their child.

Chansky (2004) reported that certain parenting styles are associated with high levels of anxiety in children, including (a) parental overcontrol, such as intrusive parenting or restricted autonomy and independence; (b) overprotection, such as excessive caution and unnecessary protective behaviors; (c) modeling of anxious interpretation, such as agreeing with the child's distortion of risk or reinforcing the idea that normal things are dangerous; (d) tolerance or encouragement of avoidance behavior, such as suggesting or agreeing with avoidance of something difficult; and (e) rejection or criticism, such as disapproving, judgmental, dismissive, or critical behavior. These styles are also likely to have an adverse impact on children with other disorders.

Establishing Realistic Expectations

Children may spend considerable time and energy coping with the symptoms of mental illness. Illness-related symptoms often vary across time and circumstances, which requires flexibility on the part of parents. Although a child's symptoms may be frustrating or disturbing to parents, it is important for parents to recognize that children often have little control over symptoms that may seem irrational to others. Parents can acknowledge the child's symptomatic behavior without encouraging or reinforcing it. Responding with impatience, criticism, or punishment may increase anxiety and exacerbate symptoms. It is important for parents to:

- Gain a better understanding of their child's illness and any limitations it might impose on home and school life;
- Develop realistic expectations regarding home and school obligations;
- Adjust expectations during crises, relapses, or periods of symptom exacerbation;
- Set clear limits when behavior is not acceptable, including behavior that is abusive, self-destructive, harmful to others, damaging to property, or severely disruptive;
- Impose consequences when those limits are exceeded; and
- Decide which behaviors can be ignored, such as behavior that is merely annoying or embarrassing.

Maintaining a Balance That Meets the Needs of All Members

Childhood mental illness can function as an energy sink that consumes family time, energy, and resources. Especially during crises, families may sometimes have difficulty fulfilling their basic functions and meeting the needs of all their members (see Marsh, 2001). Over the long term, however, parents need to:

- Nurture their family relationships;
- Assist young members of the family to accomplish their developmental tasks;
- Assist teenagers with educational and vocational plans;
- Spend quality time with their spouse or partner;
- Engage in recreational and leisure activities; and
- Plan family holidays and celebrations.

Meeting the Needs of Well Siblings

Early-onset mental illness has a profound impact on all members of the family. Yet, little attention has been paid to the needs of well siblings, who often feel like forgotten family members (Marsh & Dickens, 1997). Young family members are especially vulnerable to disruptive or traumatic events, such as the mental illness in their family. Compared with adults, children have more limited coping skills, are more dependent on other people, and have fewer psychological defenses. In addition, early developmental accomplishments provide the foundation for later ones, and delays or disruptions in development may have long-term consequences, including a residue of "unfinished business" that reverberates through future years. During adolescence, for example, teenagers must establish their sense of identity, which may be complicated by concerns about their own mental health or by social stigma.

Although there is no way to protect siblings from illness-related family stress and disruption, the negative impact of the illness may be diminished if there is special attention to sibling needs and open communication within the family. In the words of one sibling, "My parents were there for me, too, and I felt loved and valued." Practitioners can encourage parents to:

• Provide siblings with age-appropriate information about mental illness;
• Offer opportunities to ask questions and to share their feelings;
• Assure them that they are not to blame;
• Help siblings develop effective coping skills, including strategies for coping with illness-related behavior, with questions from peers, and with their own anxiety and stress;
• Provide extra support through special time with parents;
• Reassure siblings about their own mental health;
• Encourage them to participate in satisfying activities and relationships outside the family;
• Assist them in developing constructive long-range plans;
• Consider a sibling support group if one is available; and

- Consider personal counseling if well siblings experience significant distress.

Preparing for Crises

Families who are coping with early-onset mental illness may face periodic crises, such as relapses or hospitalization. To reduce the distress and disorganization that often accompany crises, parents can:

- Learn the warning signs of impending crisis, which may include sudden changes in behavior, moods, symptoms, or sleeping or eating behavior;
- Be prepared with contingency plans, emergency phone numbers, and a list of people who can offer assistance in a crisis;
- Approach the crisis in a firm, straightforward, loving, and respectful manner;
- Remain calm themselves and give the child an opportunity to calm down—a child in crisis is likely to be confused, overwhelmed, and unfocused;
- Consider a brief time-out for everyone;
- Comply with reasonable requests that are not harmful to the child or to others, which can increase the child's sense of control and support;
- Encourage everyone to sit down, which is less threatening;
- Minimize physical contact with the child, which can increase stress; and
- Avoid cornering or restricting the child, which can increase the risk of harm.

Maintaining a Hopeful Attitude

It is also essential for parents to maintain a hopeful attitude about the future, whatever the challenges in the present. Effective treatments are available for every disorder covered in this book, and legions of children and adolescents with mental illness have gone on to satisfying and productive lives as adults. In the words of one father, "Just never give up. Find ways to manage their symptoms so that they have breathing space to express themselves. Help them take small steps at their own pace. And always let them know that your love is limitless" (Foa & Andrews, 2006, p. 194). Clinicians can encourage parents to:

- Strive for a positive attitude, reframing to emphasize strengths as well as limitations and gains as well as losses;
- Maintain their sense of humor;
- Place the mental illness in perspective, as a single strand in a family tapestry woven of common bonds, memories, rituals, and celebrations;
- Find the right combination of psychosocial and psychopharmacological interventions, which may take considerable time and effort;
- Keep abreast of new developments in treatment;
- Share research findings with the child regarding effective treatments and positive outcomes;
- Encourage the child to take age-appropriate responsibility for the illness by following the treatment plan and maintaining a healthy lifestyle;
- Assist the child to acquire the knowledge, skills, and attitudes that promote positive outcomes;
- Encourage the child to explore new interests and activities; and
- Implement relapse prevention strategies, such as identifying symptom triggers, charting symptoms and moods, and using stress management techniques.

Coping With Mental Illness in School

There are many ways by which school personnel can assist children and adolescents to cope with mental illness. Working with families or with a multidisciplinary team, clinicians can assist families to obtain school-based interventions that can meet the academic, social, and psychological needs of particular children. As we discussed in Chapter 4, some children will be eligible for services or accommodations through the Individuals With Disabilities Education Act (IDEA), as spelled out in an Individualized Education Program (IEP), or through Section 504 of the Rehabilitation Act of 1973. Other children may benefit from a less formal plan designed to support them in the school setting.

As Chansky (2004) discussed, parents should provide information to school personnel about their child's difficulties, work out a system to support their child in the school setting, and establish a communication system to share information and to monitor both their child's symptoms and the effectiveness of the plan. It is important to recognize that children with mental illness should be encouraged and reinforced for functioning as normally as possible in a regular classroom. Strategies that unnecessarily highlight or reinforce symptoms or that appear to other children to offer preferential treatment are not helpful. Thus, school personnel should ensure that school-based intervention strategies are appropriate, necessary, reasonable, and beneficial. At the same time, it is important to recognize that mental illness can undermine the ability of students to function successfully in an academic environment.

As noted, diagnostic-specific intervention strategies are discussed in Chapters 7 through 10. However, a wide range of strategies may be helpful across diagnostic categories. Potential school-based interventions include becoming knowledgeable about child and adolescent mental illness, establishing a supportive school environment, implementing intervention strategies for teachers, implementing intervention strategies for schoolwork, and offering school-based mental health interventions. Working together, families, mental health professionals, and school personnel can adapt these interventions to meet the requirements of particular students, disorders, and schools.

*Becoming Knowledgeable About Child
and Adolescent Mental Illness*

School personnel can assist students by learning about mental illness, its treatment, and available services. In-service programs and professional conferences can prepare educators to identify students with mental disorders, to make appropriate referrals, and to work collaboratively with mental health providers.

Establishing a Supportive School Environment

As noted in this chapter, all children benefit from a supportive family environment, but such an environment is especially important for those with mental illness. Similarly, although all students can benefit from a supportive school environment, such an environment is essential for those with mental illness. School personnel can work to maintain a safe, structured, and consistent environment, to diminish stress within the school, and to reduce opportunities for possible bullying by others.

Implementing Intervention Strategies for Teachers

Even when school-based mental health services are not available, teachers can make a considerable difference in the lives of students with mental illness. Initially, they can cultivate a welcoming classroom environment.

- Keep the classroom free from stigma and ridicule.
- Educate students about mental illness.
- Model appropriate behavior in anxiety-provoking situations.
- Use a calm, quiet voice to reduce the student's anxiety.
- Reward the student's efforts.
- Focus on the student's strengths to combat feelings of low self-esteem.

- Focus on correct answers rather than errors.
- Assist the student to establish practical, achievable goals.
- Assist the student in prioritizing work.
- When the student's behavior is inappropriate, provide acceptable behavior choices.

In addition, teachers can monitor content to increase student engagement and to avoid exacerbating illness-related symptoms. For example, they can:

- Connect academic assignments to student-specific interests;
- Embed desirable, familiar, or safe content in instruction;
- Avoid unnecessary exposure to anxiety-provoking stimuli;
- Provide creative, safe content activities to allow the expression of ideas; or
- Add literature that addresses the student's fears or illustrates coping strategies.

Teachers can facilitate positive peer interactions to alleviate concerns for both the student and classmates.

- Allow the student to sit among familiar or preferred classmates.
- Structure class activities to facilitate inclusion of students who may be socially isolated.
- Identify specific others with whom the student can do academic tasks.
- Have the student participate in cooperative learning with peers.
- Have the student participate in social encounters assigned as part of schoolwork.

Teachers can also provide assistance when illness-related symptoms interfere with learning.

- Provide a safe place for the student to calm down (e.g., in a corner of the classroom).

- Allow the student to take a time-out when a situation is unmanageable.
- Have the student start with familiar, previously successful tasks before moving to new or more challenging tasks.
- Provide individual prompting and support in the classroom to assist the student to organize, refocus, and complete daily assignments.
- Be aware that transitions may be particularly difficult for the student and provide advance notice and extra time for moving to another task or location.
- Allow the student to discreetly accommodate needs caused by medication side effects, such as dry mouth or frequent urination.

Implementing Interventions for Schoolwork

Although students with mental illness should be encouraged to function as normally as possible, the core symptoms of mental illness can have a major impact in school. When necessary and appropriate, the following accommodations should be written into the IEP to ensure continuity in implementation of services:

- Provide a quiet area without distractions for test taking or studying.
- Allow the student to tape record homework.
- Offer a choice of projects if the student has difficulty beginning a task.
- Allow extra time to complete certain types of assignments.
- Break down tasks to make them more manageable.
- Minimize extraneous information so the student can focus on the most important material.
- Identify study partners who can support and assist with assignments.
- Grade the student based on work completed or attempted rather than work assigned.
- Adjust the homework load to prevent the student from becoming overwhelmed.

- If concentration cannot be sustained, allow the student to use appropriate aids, such as a dictionary or calculator during testing.
- Offer classroom accommodations, such as prearranged breaks, a tape recorder, a laptop computer, a calculator, a note taker, a photocopy of notes, or textbooks on tape.
- For assignments, provide substitute assignments (e.g., portfolios instead of tests), advance notice of assignments, delay in assignment due dates, alternative modes of expression (e.g., handwritten rather than typed), or alternative forms for students to demonstrate course mastery.
- For examinations, provide a change in test format (e.g., oral versus written), extended time, use of computer software programs or other technical assistance, segmented testing, increased frequency of tests, or individually proctored exams, even while in the hospital.
- Provide assignment or grade accommodations when the student has missed school due to relapses or hospitalization.
- Provide extra-credit opportunities, particularly following relapses.

Offering School-Based Mental Health Interventions

When school-based mental health services are available, schools can play an essential role in the treatment of child and adolescent mental disorders. Children with mental illness respond best when home and school environments are consistent. School personnel can collaborate with clinicians and families to support and reinforce the treatment plan and to coordinate intervention strategies used at home and in school. For example, school personnel might:

- Provide individual or group counseling to address academic, emotional, behavioral, and social issues within the school setting;
- Identify a hierarchy of safe places to go or staff to help a student calm down or obtain assistance;
- Devise specific actions to be taken when the student experiences

disruptive symptoms, such as a panic attack, a manic episode, delusions, or hallucinations;

- Provide the student with grounding activities, such as familiar, predictable activities;
- Have the student journal regularly to monitor anxiety-provoking situations or to identify mood patterns or cycles;
- Check daily with the student regarding symptoms, such as anxiety level or mood status;
- Set up a chart to record illness-related problems as they occur with a particular student;
- Provide group or peer bibliotherapy activities that address fears or topics worrisome to the student;
- Identify extracurricular activities in which the student can be with peers who have common interests;
- Modify classroom activities to reflect fluctuations in symptoms or medication side effects;
- Allow the student to have homebound instruction during relapses or periods of symptom exacerbation;
- Develop specific plans for responding to inappropriate symptom-driven behaviors to avoid suspension or expulsion;
- If relapse occurs, provide an incomplete grade rather than a failure;
- Limit the number of classes in the upper grades by making up missed classes in summer school or extending graduation by a semester or two;
- Anticipate issues, such as school avoidance, if there are unresolved social or academic problems; and
- If the student is avoiding school, determine the cause and address it, initiating a plan to return to school as quickly as possible.

School personnel can also work with students to develop effective coping skills that can enhance their functioning in the classroom and help them manage illness-related symptoms. It is important to enlist the student's help in finding strategies that can be used to achieve goals or manage symptoms.

- Assist the student to develop and use anxiety management strategies.
- Have the student identify antecedents and precipitants of anxiety.
- Encourage the student to employ images, such as a favorite place or pet, to counter anxious and disturbing feelings.
- Help the student acquire effective study skills and test-taking strategies.
- Have the student practice speaking in front of small groups before presenting to the entire class.
- Have the student rehearse social skills in a smaller or more relaxed setting.
- If appropriate, help the student enhance communication, problem-solving, and assertiveness skills (see next section).

If the treatment plan includes cognitive-behavioral therapy, school personnel can reinforce this approach. For example, the student can be encouraged to practice positive self-talk, such as "I can do this," and to identify and counter irrational and negative thoughts.

Enhancing Family Effectiveness

Much is known about family coping in general. For example, Figley (1989) identified 11 characteristics of functional family coping: clear acceptance of the stressor, a family-centered locus of problem, solution-oriented problem solving, high tolerance, clear and direct expressions of commitment and affection, open and effective communication, high family cohesion, flexible family roles, efficient resource utilization, absence of violence, and infrequent substance use. All of these characteristics are likely to enhance the family's ability to cope with mental illness. Thus, practitioners can assist families to build on their strengths and to identify and deal with any problems, such as violence or substance abuse, that may compromise their ability to function effectively.

Some skills are especially important in coping with child or adolescent mental illness, regardless of the diagnosis. Among the important generic skills are effective communication, stress management, problem-solving, and assertiveness skills. When working with families, clinicians need to highlight the importance of these skills in dealing with mental illness and to assess the skill-related strengths and limitations of particular families. Many self-help books are available for families, including *Messages: The Communication Skills Book* (McKay, Davis, & Fanning, 1995); *Relaxation & Stress Reduction Workbook* (Davis, Eshelman, & McKay, 2006); *Successful Problem Solving* (McKay & Fanning, 2002); and *The Assertiveness Workbook* (Paterson, 2000).

Communication Skills

Good communication skills are extremely important for family members. Families need to be able to communicate effectively among themselves, with professionals and other service providers, and with their child. Basic communication skills include two essential elements: effective listening, which is active, nonjudgmental, responsive, and empathic; and effective expression, which is clear, complete, direct, and supportive. In addition to these general guidelines, it is important to minimize critical and hostile communication, which may increase the level of stress.

Miklowitz and George (2008) made recommendations regarding family communication in the case of teenage depression. Suggestions for parents include:

- Listening nonjudgmentally and expressing warmth, even when the teen is angry and rejecting;
- Validating the teen's feelings of despair but expressing hope of overcoming these feelings;
- Encouraging the teen to talk about feelings but gently backing off if there is resistance;
- Highlighting even small improvements or efforts;

- Putting aside long-standing conflicts and calling a truce;
- Expressing their expectations clearly, succinctly, and calmly; and
- Asking teens if they want to hear advice before offering it.

They also recommended that parents avoid

- Giving commonsense advice, such as "pull yourself together" or "buck up and beat this thing," which will be experienced as invalidating;
- Taking the teen's anger and hostility personally; it is usually the illness talking;
- Expressing significant anxiety about the teen's mood state and where it will lead;
- Saying things that the teen will experience as a guilt trip;
- Discussing their own or another family member's depression or suicidal feelings in front of the teen; and
- Allowing the teen to get embroiled in conflicts between parents.

Stress Management Skills

In addition, given the stress and disruption that accompany mental illness, family members need good stress management skills. Families can learn to manage stress more effectively by understanding the nature, kinds, and sources of stressors in their lives and by developing more effective strategies for managing stress. When working with individual families, practitioners can assist them to acquire stress management strategies that meet their needs. Clinicians can describe the wide range of strategies that are available, mention some helpful resources (e.g., Davis et al., 2006), explain that there are individual differences in the preference for particular strategies, and demonstrate some techniques. These might include progressive muscle relaxation, visualization of a peaceful scene, breathing exercises, and meditation. Families might also be encouraged to begin an exercise program, which is one of the most effective methods of reducing stress.

Problem-Solving Skills

Families also need good problem-solving and conflict management skills since mental illness creates fertile ground for disagreement. Especially at the onset of the illness, family members may disagree about the nature of the child's problems, the probable causes, the treatment plan, and the best way to manage symptoms. Professionals who fail to provide sufficient information to families may heighten these differences. Good problem-solving and conflict management skills may improve their ability to resolve issues within the family and with service providers. When problems or conflicts involve other people, it is essential that the process take place in an atmosphere of mutual tolerance and respect.

Clinicians can assist families to understand and implement effective problem-solving skills by working with them on a current problem. Mueser and Gingerich (2006) provided a useful model of problem solving in mental illness. Their step-by-step-method involves the following:

Step 1: Define the problem, which involves specifying the problem and what the family wants to achieve.

Step 2: Generate possible solutions, which involves brainstorming as many solutions as possible without evaluating or criticizing them at this point.

Step 3: Evaluate the advantages and disadvantages of each solution.

Step 4: Choose the best solution, considering its practicality, its probable impact on the defined problem, and the resources needed to implement it.

Step 5: Plan how to carry out the best solution, which involves breaking down the solution into specific steps and assigning someone to carry out each step.

Step 6: Evaluate whether the solution was implemented and the problem solved.

If the solution has not been effective in solving the problem, the process can begin again with the consideration of other solutions that can be used.

Assertiveness Skills

Assertiveness is also an essential skill for family members, who need to be able to stand up for their legitimate rights, to refuse to allow others to take advantage of them, and to communicate their desires in an open, direct, and appropriate manner. Assertive families meet their own needs without violating the rights of others. In contrast, family members should avoid passive strategies that meet the needs of others at their own expense and aggressive strategies that meet their needs at the expense of others. On a long-term basis, neither of these strategies is effective. Passivity is likely to leave them angry and resentful; aggression is likely to alienate others.

HELPING FAMILIES COPE WITH SPECIFIC MENTAL DISORDERS

CHAPTER SEVEN

Talking to Families
About Anxiety Disorders

Even as an infant, Luis Martinez was fretful and restless. During elementary school, he seemed to worry more than other children. In middle school, Luis often complained of stomachaches, problems concentrating in school, and difficulty going to sleep at night. Noticing that he always seemed tense and irritable, his mother, Rosa, asked Luis what was bothering him. He responded that he didn't know, but said he couldn't stop worrying. Rosa was concerned and spoke with his pediatrician, who reminded her that Luis had always been a worrier and suggested they wait and see if he improved. Within a few months, however, he developed new symptoms, including repeated handwashing and an excessive fear of germs and contamination. When his father, Carlos, insisted that he stop washing his hands so often, Luis responded that he couldn't help it, frustrating and confusing his parents. Rosa could see that her son seemed driven to perform the handwashing and again contacted his pediatrician, who recognized the symptoms of obsessive-compulsive disorder (OCD) and made a referral to the local mental health center, which couldn't give

Luis an appointment for 6 weeks. In the meantime, Carlos became increasingly angry with Luis, demanding that he stop his "foolish" behavior. In turn, Luis became even more anxious and appeared trapped in a pattern of behavior that seemed senseless to him as well. Rosa tried without success to reduce the tension in the home and to reassure her other children.

In this chapter, we focus on anxiety disorders and provide the basic information that families need. What these disorders have in common is the presence of intense fear, worry, or uneasiness that can shadow the lives of children and significantly affect their lives. The Substance Abuse and Mental Health Services Administration (SAMHSA) Web site (http://mentalhealth.samhsa.gov/) reports that anxiety disorders are among the most common mental, emotional, and behavioral problems to occur during childhood and adolescence, affecting about 13 of every 100 young people. Girls experience anxiety disorders more frequently than boys.

About half of those with an anxiety disorder have a second anxiety disorder or other mental disorder, such as depression. As SAMHSA (2003) pointed out, if not treated early, anxiety disorders can lead to problems with school attendance and performance, impaired relations with peers, low self-esteem, alcohol or other drug use, and continuing problems that affect adult functioning. Anxiety disorders are also the most prevalent mental disorder in adults, who typically report that their symptoms started in childhood (Chansky, 2004). Fortunately, effective treatments are available for all of the anxiety disorders.

We begin with the diagnostic criteria for the major anxiety disorders. Other topics include risk factors, treatment, and coping strategies for home and school. We then return to Luis Martinez and his family and offer some possible interventions as well as an illustrative session with his parents.

Diagnostic Criteria for Anxiety Disorders

As specified in the text revision of the *Diagnostic and Statistical Manual of Mental Disorders, Fourth Edition* (*DSM-IV-TR*; American Psychiatric Association, 2000), anxiety disorders include generalized anxiety disorder, panic disorder, phobias, OCD, separation anxiety disorder, and posttraumatic stress disorder. Because comorbidity with other anxiety disorders is common, families may benefit from a brief overview of the different types of anxiety disorders.

Generalized Anxiety Disorder

Children with generalized anxiety disorder experience excessive and persistent worry about events or activities in their daily lives. They may worry about matters pertaining to school, sports, health, and family; they have difficulty controlling their anxiety; and they often seek reassurance from parents. Anxiety-related symptoms may include restlessness, fatigue, difficulty concentrating, irritability, muscle tension, and sleep disturbance.

Panic Disorder

Panic disorder is characterized by recurrent, unexpected panic attacks, which are discrete periods of intense fear or discomfort. Symptoms may include pounding heart, sweating, trembling, shortness of breath, a feeling of choking, chest pain, nausea, and dizziness. Panic attacks are often marked by a sense of impending doom and a fear of losing control or "going crazy." Panic attacks may occur with other anxiety disorders.

Phobias

Children who have phobias manifest marked and persistent fear of a specific object or situation, such as animals or a specific type of animal, heights, storms, water, enclosed spaces, or medical procedures. Adults recognize that the fear is excessive or unreasonable, although this feature may be absent in children, who may express their anxiety by crying, tantrums, freezing, or clinging. The phobic situation is often avoided, but may be endured with intense anxiety or distress. Social phobia is marked by persistent fear of social or performance situations in which embarrassment may occur.

Obsessive-Compulsive Disorder

Obsessive-compulsive disorder (OCD) is distinguished by recurrent obsessions or compulsions that are severe enough to be time consuming or to cause significant distress or impairment. *Obsessions* are recurrent and persistent ideas, thoughts, impulses, or images that cause marked anxiety or distress and are experienced as intrusive and inappropriate, although children may not recognize them as excessive or unreasonable. The most common obsessions are repeated thoughts about contamination, repeated doubts, a need to have things in a particular order, aggressive or horrific impulses, and sexual imagery. The person typically attempts to ignore or suppress such obsessions or to neutralize them with some other thought or action.

Compulsions are repetitive behaviors or mental acts that the individual feels driven to perform in response to an obsession or according to rules that must be applied rigidly. The behaviors or mental acts are aimed at preventing or reducing distress or preventing some dreaded event or situation. Common repetitive behaviors involve handwashing, ordering, and checking. Mental acts may include praying, counting, or repeating words silently.

Separation Anxiety Disorder

Separation anxiety disorder is characterized by developmentally inappropriate and excessive anxiety concerning separation from the home or from major attachment figures. Symptoms may include persistent and excessive worry about major attachment figures or potential separation, persistent reluctance or refusal to go to school, persistent reluctance to be alone or without major attachment figures, persistent reluctance or refusal to go to sleep in the absence of a major attachment figure, and repeated complaints of physical symptoms when separation occurs or is anticipated.

Posttraumatic Stress Disorder

The essential feature of posttraumatic stress disorder is exposure to a traumatic event that involved actual or threatened death or serious injury to oneself or others and that evoked feelings of intense fear, helplessness, or horror, which may be manifested in children by disorganized or agitated behavior. Characteristic symptoms include persistent reexperiencing of the traumatic event, persistent avoidance of stimuli associated with the trauma, numbing of general responsiveness, and persistent symptoms of increased arousal. Symptoms must cause clinically significant distress or impairment in important areas of functioning. If the duration of symptoms is less than 3 months, the diagnosis is acute stress disorder.

Risk Factors

There is general agreement that anxiety disorders involve the interaction of multiple risk factors (Chansky, 2004; Foa & Andrews, 2006; Rapee, Spence, Cobham, & Wignall, 2000). Important risk factors include:

- Genetic factors, which determine the overall vulnerability to anxiety;
- Neurobiological factors, such as abnormal brain structure or function;
- Other biological factors, such as the subtype of OCD called pediatric

autoimmune neuropsychiatric disorders associated with streptococcal infections (PANDAS);
- Temperament, such as greater sensitivity or lower distress tolerance;
- Parenting style, such as overcontrol or overprotection;
- Modeling, such as a caregiver who manifests excessive anxiety; and
- Environmental factors, such as serious illness, death of a loved one, exposure to violence, or family disruption due to separation or divorce.

Each of these risk factors can also serve as a protective factor that reduces the likelihood of an anxiety disorder, such as an easygoing temperament, healthy parental role models, and a supportive family environment. Other sections discuss strategies that can help families minimize risk factors and strengthen protective factors. Some factors are relatively enduring, such as genetics and temperament, although practitioners can help parents to understand and adapt to their child's unique personality. Clinicians can work with parents to modify other factors associated with high anxiety in children, such as parenting style or family stress.

Treatment

Anxiety disorders are among the most treatable mental disorders. Indeed, many empirical studies have demonstrated the effectiveness of cognitive-behavioral therapy (CBT), which is the most widely used treatment for childhood anxiety disorders (Haugaard, 2008). Depending on the specific disorder and symptoms, the following CBT strategies may be appropriate:

- Cognitive therapy, which involves identifying and replacing negative or anxiety-producing thoughts with more realistic thoughts;
- Behavior therapy, which targets the symptoms of the disorder, such

as the use of systematic desensitization in the treatment of phobias and the use of reinforcement to reduce avoidance behavior and enhance coping strategies;

- Exposure therapy, which involves gradually confronting the anxiety-provoking situation until it no longer evokes extreme distress;
- Response prevention, such as delaying compulsive handwashing;
- Anxiety management, which involves building skills to reduce anxiety through progressive muscle relaxation, deep breathing, stress inoculation, guided visualization, thought stopping, and other strategies;
- Skills building, which is designed to strengthen coping skills, such as problem solving, assertiveness, and positive self-talk; and
- Relapse prevention, which is designed to identify possible anxiety-provoking situations and develop strategies for lessening the anxiety response.

In addition, child and adolescent interventions generally include family psychoeducation, which is designed to offer education about anxiety disorders and their treatment, to strengthen coping skills, and to support family members. Depending on the specific disorder and the unique characteristics of the child and family, other treatments may be appropriate, such as the use of parent management training for separation anxiety disorder, or of eye movement desensitization and reprocessing (EMDR) for posttraumatic stress disorder.

In general, CBT is the initial treatment of choice for children with anxiety disorders because it is empirically supported and least invasive, with no negative side effects. In some cases, however, medication may be appropriate, such as when the symptoms cause extreme distress, severely undermine the child's ability to function at home or in school, or prevent the use of CBT. Medication may also be added if there has been no response to psychosocial intervention within a reasonable time period.

The most common medications used to treat anxiety disorders are in the class of antidepressants known as selective serotonin reuptake inhibitors (SSRIs). These medications, which include Celexa, Lexapro, Luvox, Paxil, Prozac, and Zoloft, have been used effectively for generalized anxiety disorder, panic disorder, obsessive-compulsive disorder, social anxiety, and separation anxiety disorder. Most medication studies have been conducted with adults, but recent studies of SSRIs have shown promise with children (Chansky, 2004). Writing about the treatment of OCD, Wagner (2002a) reported that the combination of CBT and medication is considered more effective than either option alone, that about 40% of those who do not respond to one medication have a good chance of responding to another one, and that obsessive-compulsive symptoms usually return when medication is discontinued.

Given the media attention to concerns about the increased risk of suicide associated with the use of SSRI antidepressants for children, families are likely to have questions about these medications. In 2004, the Food and Drug Administration (FDA) issued a public warning about an increased risk of suicidal thoughts or behavior in children and adolescents treated with SSRI medications and adopted a "black box" warning indicating the risk. The National Institute of Mental Health (2008) reported results of a comprehensive review of pediatric trials conducted between 1988 and 2006. This meta-analysis suggested the benefits of antidepressant medications likely outweigh their risks to children and adolescents with anxiety disorders. No completed suicides occurred in children treated with SSRI medications, although about 4% experienced suicidal thinking or behavior, including actual suicide attempts (twice the rate of those taking placebos).

If antidepressants are prescribed for children with anxiety disorders, practitioners should share these research findings with parents in a discussion of the potential risks and benefits of medication as well as the risks of undertaking no psychopharmacological treatment. If a course of medication is undertaken, children should be carefully monitored for side effects and complications, including the possible presence of suicidal ideation and behavior.

Helping Families Cope With Anxiety Disorders

Many resources are available for families who include a child or adolescent with an anxiety disorder. One excellent book, *If Your Adolescent Has an Anxiety Disorder* (Foa & Andrews, 2006), provides current information about anxiety disorders in general as well as disorder-specific suggestions. Other books that focus on anxiety disorders include *The Anxiety Cure for Kids: A Guide for Parents* (Spencer, DuPont, & DuPont, 2003); *Freeing Your Child From Anxiety* (Chansky, 2004); *Helping Your Anxious Child: A Step-by-Step Guide for Parents* (Rapee et al., 2000); and *Worried No More: Help and Hope for Anxious Children* (Wagner, 2002b).

Other resources include workbooks for children and adolescents themselves, including *The Anxiety Workbook for Teens* (Schab, 2008); *I Bet I Won't Fret* (Sisemore, 2007); *What to Do When You Worry Too Much* (Heubner, 2006); and *What To Do When You're Scared & Worried: A Guide for Kids* (Crist, 2004). The workbooks for children, which are designed to be used with parents, include a range of exercises that help children understand anxiety, manage their fears and worries, identify and counter irrational fears, and develop effective coping skills. Books for adolescents offer similar material designed to be used by teenagers.

In addition, some resources focus on specific anxiety disorders, including *Helping Your Child Overcome Separation Anxiety or School Refusal: A Step-by-Step Guide for Parents* (Eisen & Engler, 2006) and *Say Goodbye to Being Shy* (Brozovich & Chase, 2008), which may be helpful for social anxiety. Several useful books are available for OCD, including *Freeing Your Child From Obsessive-Compulsive Disorder* (Chansky, 2000); *Helping Your Child With OCD* (Fitzgibbons & Pedrick, 2003); *The OCD Workbook* (Hyman & Pedrick, 2005); *Up and Down the Worry Hill: A Children's Book About Obsessive-Compulsive Disorder and Its Treatment* (Wagner & Jutton, 2004); and *What to Do When Your Child Has Obsessive-Compulsive Disorder* (Wagner, 2002a).

Many self-help books written for adults with anxiety disorders may also be adapted for children and adolescents, such as those published by New Harbinger (http://www.newharbinger.com/), which offers adult-oriented books on stress management, anxiety and phobia, cognitive-behavioral techniques, trauma and abuse, OCD, and a range of other topics. For example, *The Anxiety & Phobia Workbook* (Bourne, 2005) covers relaxation, exercise, coping with panic, exposure, overcoming negative self-talk, changing mistaken beliefs, visualization, self-esteem, nutrition, medication, meditation techniques, and anxiety-triggering health conditions. Parents of young children can review the material, discuss it with their child's therapist, and decide what works best for their child and family. Likewise, adolescents may find books written for adults very helpful in understanding and coping with their anxiety disorder.

Because anxiety disorders generally affect functioning in multiple domains, it is essential for clinicians to work with the family, including the child or adolescent, in developing a comprehensive treatment plan that specifies and coordinates home- and school-based interventions. Parents and children who play an active role in designing the treatment plan are more likely to accept and support the plan. Effective collaboration and coordination among the clinician, family, and school—what has been called the *home–school–agency triangle* (Cook-Morales, 2002)—establishes a team that can maintain a consistent and supportive environment for the child; coordinate clinic-, home-, and school-based intervention strategies; and monitor the course of the disorder and the effectiveness of treatment.

The specific home- and school-based interventions will depend on the treatment plan, the unique characteristics of the child and family, and the resources available through the school. Some parents and children may welcome an active role in treatment and respond well to homework assignments and exercises; others may prefer less involvement. If a child has an Individualized Education Program (IEP), the plan will spell out the accommodations and interventions that will be provided to remedy educational deficits. If there has been no formal special education process, families may work more informally with teachers and other school personnel.

We offer a range of possible home- and school-based interventions that can be adapted to particular children, families, practitioners, and settings. Some strategies can be implemented in both home and school settings, such as behavioral strategies, which are effective in treating many anxiety-related symptoms. The Massachusetts General Hospital School Psychiatry Program & MADI Resource Center (http://www .massgeneral.org/schoolpsychiatry/) provides a useful discussion of behavioral strategies. Parents or teachers might implement a chart system in which a certain number of stars may be "cashed in" for a reward. Behavioral plans offer many advantages. For example, such plans reward good behavior rather than punish misbehavior, provide frequent acknowledgments of success, reinforce the child for making an effort to reduce problem behaviors, and develop meaningful incentives with the child, such as praise, gold stars on a chart, special time with a parent, or a trip for ice cream.

Helping Children Cope With Anxiety Disorders at Home

As noted, certain parenting styles and behaviors are associated with high levels of anxiety in children, including parental overcontrol, overprotection, and modeling. Clinicians can educate parents about the importance of goodness of fit and, if appropriate, assist them to recognize and modify their own parenting style. For example, it is generally not helpful for parents to

- Tell the child to stop worrying, which is not always possible.
- Respond to anxiety-related symptoms with advice and logic, because such symptoms are by their nature excessive or illogical.
- Offer too much reassurance, which provides only temporary relief.
- Participate in anxiety-related rituals or behavior, which may reinforce the symptoms.

- Step in to protect the child from an anxiety-provoking situation, which prevents the child from confronting the fear.
- Respond with impatience, criticism, scolding, or punishment, which may increase anxiety and encourage the child to hide symptoms.

On the other hand, there are many parenting strategies that can serve as a buffer for children with anxiety disorders. In the following sections, we offer suggestions for helping children cope with anxiety disorders at home and in school; these suggestions are based on several publications (see Chansky, 2004; Foa & Andrews, 2006; Rapee et al., 2000; Wagner, 2002a) as well as other resources, such as the Web site of the Massachusetts General Hospital School Psychiatry Program & Madi Resource Center (http://www.massgeneral.org/schoolpsy chiatry/).

Both parents and children should be encouraged to play an active role in developing home-based interventions and to share their observations about what is most helpful. These interventions should complement those specified in the treatment plan and be acceptable to families. Here are some suggestions that can be discussed with parents:

- Keep calm when the child becomes anxious about a situation.
- Restrict anxiety-provoking television programs and video games.
- Relabel the problem as a symptom of the disorder (e.g., "it's the OCD talking").
- Avoid abruptly making changes and new rules, which can cause upheaval in children who have difficulty with transitions.
- Plan for transitions, such as getting to school in the morning or preparing for bed in the evening, which may be complicated by fears and anxieties.
- Extinguish excessively anxious behavior by ignoring the behavior or responding with less concern.
- Discourage avoidance behavior and gently encourage the child to approach the fearful object or situation.

- Provide a low-key reminder that the child has survived prior anxiety-provoking situations.
- Talk about nonemotionally charged issues (e.g., a pet, a sports team).
- Following a traumatic event, let the child know you are available when he or she needs to talk, but avoid forcing a discussion.
- In cases of school refusal, support the child's quick return to school.

In working with the therapist, parents can play an active role in treatment by implementing interventions at home that assist their child to develop effective coping strategies. Here are some home-based interventions that incorporate cognitive-behavioral and other effective strategies:

- Implement a token economy that specifies realistic goals and the rewards that can be earned, such as stars on a chart, special time with parents, or small toys.
- Teach relaxation techniques, such as deep breathing, progressive relaxation, counting to 10, or visualizing a calm place.
- Join the child in using coping strategies (e.g., "Let's do our breathing exercise together").
- Encourage the child to use self-calming strategies, such as comfort objects (e.g., a favorite toy or stuffed animal).
- Encourage the child to use grounding strategies to counter high levels of anxiety, such as focusing on the room (e.g., describe its contents, touch the chair, walk around the room).
- Encourage creative activities, such as writing, drawing, or listening to music.
- Develop a timetable for dealing with anxiety-provoking concerns (e.g., "Let's talk about how we can help you sleep in your own room with just a small nightlight when you turn 5 next month").
- Make a hierarchy of anxiety-provoking situations with the child, what Chansky (2004) has called the "stairs of learning."

- Rate each situation with a "fearometer" (Wagner, 2002a), based on an anxiety scale of 1 (*no problem*) to 10 (*extremely hard*).
- Help the child approach fears using gradual exposure, which involves moving in small sequential steps from the least-feared situation to the most anxiety-provoking situation.
- If the child is too fearful to approach the actual situation, begin with images of the feared object or situation, such as pictures or photographs.
- Work with the child to develop realistic goals, determining the "comfort zone" and small steps that increase the likelihood of success.
- Practice realistic thinking and supportive self-talk with the child, beginning with irrational thoughts and developing more appropriate responses.
- Help the child talk back to the anxious thoughts or behaviors (e.g., "My parents always come home, so I can stay with the babysitter").
- Help the child find alternative thoughts or behaviors (e.g., "I can raise my hand in class and ask my teacher a question").
- Help the child reduce the anxiety-related behavior (e.g., washing hands for 5 minutes instead of 10).
- Use role-playing with puppets, dolls, or stuffed animals to help children approach anxiety-provoking situations.
- Identify an incompatible behavior that can be used to block the unwanted response (e.g., going for a walk instead of washing hands).
- Provide social skills training for children who are excessively shy or have social phobia, using prompting, role-playing, gentle feedback, and praise to enhance nonverbal communication, voice quality, conversation skills, friendship skills, and assertiveness (see Rapee et al., 2000).
- Set aside two 15-minute periods for worrying each day, which sets boundaries for worries rather than letting them run rampant (Foa & Andrews, 2006).

Helping Children Cope With Anxiety Disorders in School

Working with families or with a multidisciplinary team, clinicians can encourage the development and implementation of school-based interventions that can meet the needs of particular students with anxiety disorders. These may include services or accommodations specified in an IEP or a less formal plan designed to support them in the school setting. In any case, families should establish a collaborative partnership with the school to share information and to monitor their child's symptoms and progress.

In Chapter 6, we discussed a range of school-based interventions that can be adapted for particular students, disorders, and schools. In this chapter, we focus on interventions that specifically focus on anxiety disorders. Some of the following school-based interventions are appropriate for anxiety disorders in general; others are helpful for specific anxiety disorders. As noted, students with mental illness should be encouraged to function as normally as possible in a regular classroom. Thus, the goal is to design school-based services that are necessary, appropriate, reasonable, and beneficial.

Foa and Andrews (2006) offered potential school-based interventions for specific anxiety disorders. For social anxiety disorder, they suggested that teachers explain that public speaking gets easier with practice, look for ways to involve everyone in group activities, gently prompt the student to join in class discussions, privately praise the student for speaking up, avoid punishing or shaming the student for not speaking, and include formal training in public speaking as part of the classroom curriculum.

For generalized anxiety disorder, teachers might put limits on revisions or erasures, set time limits for turning in assignments, help students realistically assess the probability of a bad outcome, encourage realistic thinking about the consequences of a minor mistake, taper off the amount of reassurance provided, and serve as a positive role model.

For OCD, Foa and Andrews (2006) suggested that teachers deal with contamination symptoms and washing compulsions by allowing students to be first in line at the cafeteria, seating students where they are the first to receive handouts, giving students an extra set of "uncontaminated" books to keep at home, permitting students to avoid crowded hallways by going to their lockers early, allowing students to go to the bathroom whenever they feel the need, and limiting the number of bathroom passes when students are ready. For obsessions and compulsions that lead to perfection, teachers might let students make check marks instead of filling in circles on tests and permit assignments to be typed or recorded rather than handwritten. Students who are slowed by their obsessions and compulsions might benefit from extra time for completing tests and homework and from shorter reading passages.

For posttraumatic stress disorder, Foa and Andrews (2006) recommended that teachers encourage students to express their feelings through conversation, creative writing, and art projects; provide information and answer questions about the traumatic event, without dwelling on every detail; respect the preferences of students who choose not to take part in classroom discussions about the event; help students feel safely in control of their environment by offering opportunities to make decisions in the classroom; and reduce expectations temporarily, perhaps by giving less-demanding assignments or rescheduling papers and tests.

School personnel can also consider other strategies for students with anxiety disorders. For example, they can encourage the student to use anxiety management strategies, set up a chart to monitor anxiety-related problems as they occur in school, encourage the student to identify antecedents and precipitants of anxiety, and develop an action plan to counter significant anxiety when it occurs. In addition, some students may benefit from social skills training designed to help them expand and improve peer interactions or from cognitive-behavioral strategies that can counter irrational or negative thoughts.

Luis Martinez: The Treatment Plan

Returning to Luis Martinez and his family, Luis has already received a diagnosis of OCD. As specified in the treatment plan, the long-term goals are to assist Luis and his family to understand and accept his obsessive-compulsive disorder, to engage them in the treatment plan, to help them manage the symptoms of the disorder, and to support Luis in achieving his personal objectives. His individualized treatment plan might include the following interventions:

- Refer Luis for a medication consult to determine if he is an appropriate candidate for medication.
- Provide family psychoeducation for the Martinez family to educate them about OCD and its treatment, to strengthen their coping skills, and to offer support.
- Teach Luis anxiety management skills.
- Provide cognitive therapy to identify and replace anxiety-producing thoughts with more realistic thoughts.
- Provide exposure therapy to expose Luis gradually to anxiety-provoking situations until they no longer evoke extreme distress.
- Provide response prevention therapy to increasingly delay his compulsive handwashing.
- Work with Luis and his parents to implement these strategies at home.
- Collaborate with the school in developing an IEP that implements the anxiety management and response prevention plans used at home, provides a quiet area without distractions for test taking and studying, substitutes alternatives for assignments that are excessively anxiety-provoking, specifies a hierarchy of safe places Luis can use to calm down, and provides weekly sessions with a school counselor to help him manage school-related stress.

In addition, following family assessment, the practitioner can meet with the Martinez family to develop a family service plan designed to assist them in identifying and prioritizing their needs, in dealing with illness-related concerns, in making an informed choice about their use of other available services, and in resolving other problems in the family. For example, the family might request several sessions to help Luis's siblings deal with their questions and concerns, as well as marital therapy to help his parents manage illness-related conflict.

Working With the Martinez Family

Psychologist Elizabeth Massimo is a member of the children's team at a local mental health center. She has arranged a meeting with Rosa and Carlos Martinez to discuss results of the team's evaluation of Luis.

Dr. Massimo: Good morning, Mr. and Mrs. Martinez. Thank you for coming in. I'm Dr. Massimo, the psychologist with the children's team at the center. You've already met Dr. Goodman, our psychiatrist, and Sarah Ramos, our social worker. Our team always works closely with families, and we want to make sure we meet your needs. I'd like to begin with the results of our evaluation and then turn to our recommendations for treatment. Do you have any questions before we begin?

Rosa: I do have some questions, but they can wait until later.

Carlos: If Luis would just stop washing his hands so often, we wouldn't even need an evaluation.

Dr. Massimo: I understand how you feel, Mr. Martinez. Many family members share your frustration over behavior that persists even though it seems to make little sense. Actually, Luis shares your frustration and confusion about his behavior, which seems senseless to him as well. Luis's handwashing is a symptom of obsessive-compulsive disorder or OCD, which is an anxiety disorder. Obsessions, such as his fear of germs and contamination, are persistent thoughts that cause significant anxiety and distress—for families as well as individuals. Compulsions, such as Luis's handwashing, are repetitive behaviors that individuals with OCD feel driven to perform in response to their obsessions. Anxiety disorders are among the most common mental health problems to occur during childhood, and they are also among the most treatable.

Carlos: I don't understand why he can't just stop his foolish behavior.

Dr. Massimo: Like Luis, most people with OCD do realize their behavior is irrational, but they are unable to control themselves. Fortunately, we do have treatments that can help people with OCD to control their symptoms.

Rosa: I am so glad he can be helped. This has been extremely difficult for all of us, including our other children. It's as if Luis's problems have taken over our lives. We all feel stressed and anxious.

Dr. Massimo: I'm sure this has been very difficult for your family, as it would be for any family, but we do have effective treatments for OCD, so there is every reason to expect that Luis will improve. We sometimes talk about evidence-based treatments, which simply means that researchers have demonstrated that certain treatments are effective for particular disorders. In the case of OCD, we have two evidence-based treatments: medication and cognitive-behavioral therapy. Given the severity of Luis' symptoms, our psychiatrist believes Luis is a good candidate for an antidepressant medication that can eliminate or reduce his OCD symptoms. Most people are helped significantly by this medication. I've brought some written materials for you that describe the medication, summarize the research findings, and state the potential benefits and risks. Once you've had a chance to look over the materials, we can meet again so I can answer your questions. If you decide to follow our recommendation, we'll need your help in determining how well the medication is working. In addition to the antidepressant, we plan to help Luis learn to manage his symptoms. We generally use a range of cognitive-behavioral strategies, including anxiety management to reduce his distress, cognitive therapy to help him develop more realistic thoughts about germs and contamination, exposure therapy to gradually expose Luis to anxiety-provoking situations until they no longer evoke extreme distress, and response prevention therapy to increasingly delay his compulsive handwashing. We also want to assist you to learn how to help Luis cope with his OCD at home. I have some written materials about these cognitive-behavioral strategies. I realize this is a lot of information—you must feel a bit overwhelmed at this point.

Rosa: I do feel overwhelmed—there's so much to learn. But I'm also relieved that Luis can be helped.

Carlos: And I appreciate your taking the time to explain that Luis has OCD and really can't control his symptoms. I regret I was so impatient with him.

Dr. Massimo: Mr. Martinez, your reaction is understandable, so there's no need to feel guilty. You were just trying to help him but didn't know how. We'll work with both of you and with Luis to help him deal with his OCD. In fact, we've already begun working with Luis, who is reporting some improvement in his symptoms.

Rosa: Dr. Massimo, I'm really worried about Luis's grades, which have been getting worse. He says he has trouble concentrating and sometimes gets so anxious he can't think.

Dr. Massimo: That's very common with OCD. Our social worker would like to meet with you to discuss how we can work with the school because Luis may be eligible for special education services. She'll explain how the process works and attend meetings with you if you like. She can also share results of our evaluation with the school so a plan can be developed for helping Luis. It will be best if we all work as a team to make sure we meet Luis's needs at home and in school.

Rosa: That sounds wonderful. For the first time in months, I'm beginning to believe things will get better for Luis—and for us.

Dr. Massimo: Let's see what else we can do to help your family. You mentioned that your other children have been upset by Luis's behavior. Would you like me to set up a meeting with them to explain OCD and share the treatment plan?

Rosa: I think that would be very helpful.

Carlos: To be honest with you, I really have trouble when Luis starts his handwashing. I can't help feeling frustrated and angry. And then I get angry with Rosa when she tries to defend Luis. I know that's not helpful for any of us.

Dr. Massimo: Let's talk about that during our next meeting. As I mentioned, these are normal reactions among family members. We can talk about other ways of responding to Luis's symptoms. Now, let's speak to the receptionist about setting up the appointments we've discussed. I also want to give you contact information if you need to reach us between appointments. I look forward to working with Luis and the rest of your family.

CHAPTER EIGHT

Talking to Families About Depression

Until adolescence, Patrice Finley appeared to have few problems. She did well in school, had many friends, and enjoyed sports. Her parents, Jocelyn and Jamal, said they first noticed a change during the eighth grade. Patrice lost interest in her friends and sports, always seemed tired and listless, and spent most of her time alone in her room or asleep. She had frequent absences from school, and her grades began to drop. Her grandmother, Sharise, who lived with the family and was close to the children, told her parents that Patrice often thought about death and sometimes could not find a reason to go on living. Patrice's siblings, Jerome and Edward, were also worried about their sister. Jerome complained that Patrice had changed from a happy, outgoing sister to someone who did not care about anyone or anything.

This chapter focuses on childhood depression, which is categorized as a mood disorder along with bipolar disorder, the topic of Chapter 9. Mood disorders in children have been recognized only relatively recently, beginning in the 1970s and 1980s (Fristad & Arnold, 2004). In fact, according to the Substance Abuse and Mental Health Services Administration (SAMHSA; http://mentalhealth.samhsa.gov/), at any point in time about 5% of children and adolescents may have depression, which can have a profound impact on these young people and their families. Moreover, by the age of 18, as many as 15% to 20% of adolescents have experienced a major depressive episode (Rosenbaum & Colvino, 2008). Beginning in adolescence, females are significantly more likely than males to experience depression.

Unfortunately, although effective treatments are available for depression, a majority of these children receive no treatment at all. Untreated depression can result in a cascade of negative consequences, including an increased risk of suicide. Indeed, as we have noted, suicide is the third leading cause of death among young people aged 15 to 24 and the sixth leading cause of death among children aged 5 to 14. Fristad and Arnold (2004) discussed some of the reasons for this neglect, including the beliefs that children do not get depressed, that it is normal for adolescents to be moody, and that depression will go away quickly on its own. Thus, clinicians have an opportunity to counter these misperceptions, to assist families obtain accurate information about depression and its treatment, and to help families cope effectively with childhood depression.

Initially, we discuss the diagnostic criteria for depressive disorders. Additional topics include risk factors for depression, treatment, suicide prevention, and coping strategies for home and school. Finally, we return to Patrice Finley and her family, offer some possible interventions, and present an illustrative session with her parents.

Diagnostic Criteria for Depression

According to the *Diagnostic and Statistical Manual of Mental Disorders, Fourth Edition, Text Revision* (*DSM-IV-TR*; American Psychiatric Association, 2000), there are two depressive disorders: major depression and dysthymia. Symptoms of major depression may include despondent mood, markedly diminished interest or pleasure in activities, significant weight loss or gain, insomnia or hypersomnia, psychomotor agitation or retardation, fatigue or loss of energy, feelings of worthlessness or inappropriate guilt, diminished ability to think or concentrate, and recurrent thoughts of death or suicide. These symptoms are persistent and cause significant distress or impairment in functioning. In contrast to adults, children and adolescents may exhibit irritable rather than depressed mood, and their expected weight gain should be considered along with significant weight loss or gain. Seasonal affective disorder is distinguished by depressive symptoms at particular times of the year.

Dysthymic disorder is marked by a chronically depressed mood. Symptoms may include poor appetite or overeating, insomnia or hypersomnia, low energy or fatigue, low self-esteem, poor concentration or difficulty making decisions, and feelings of hopelessness. As with major depression, children and adolescents may experience irritable rather than depressed mood. Although the two disorders share similar symptoms, dysthymia is less severe, chronic, and persistent.

Clinicians may also see children and adolescents who are depressed in response to life events, such as the death or chronic illness of a family member, parental divorce or separation, or other distressing events, such as academic failure or termination of a romantic relationship. If the reactive depression is severe, the child may be diagnosed with adjustment disorder with depressed mood. In other cases, the depressive symptoms may be relatively mild and transitory but may still be a focus of treatment.

From the perspective of families, it is important for clinicians to discuss the different types of depression as well as their implications for children and families. For example, a single episode of major depression can last from 7 to 9 months (an entire school year), and about 40% of children who have had a single depressive episode will have another one within 2 years, and about 70% within 5 years (Fristad & Arnold, 2004). Moreover, the recurrent thoughts of death or suicide that may occur in major depression increase the risk of a suicide attempt.

Risk Factors

Families often ask what has caused their child's depression, and thus can benefit from a discussion of the relevant risk factors. As with most childhood mental disorders, the etiological picture is a complex one that involves biological, psychological, and social factors (e.g., Barnard, 2003; Haugaard, 2008). These include:

- Genetic factors because mood disorders tend to run in families;
- Neurochemical factors, such as neurotransmitter abnormalities;
- Environmental factors, such as family or academic problems;
- Health-related factors, such as illness, medication side effects, or substance abuse; and
- Cognitive factors, such as automatic or irrational negative thoughts.

Often, these factors interact in childhood depression, as in the case of a child with a family history of depression who is faced with parental separation or divorce. The child's perception of circumstances also plays an important role. Appraising the same event, for example, one child might view it as a challenge, another as an insurmountable barrier.

These variables can also serve as protective factors that reduce the risk of childhood depression or buffer its impact. For example, children who are vulnerable to depression are likely to benefit from a stable and supportive home environment, resolution of health-related problems, and a satisfying academic and social life. In addition, some personality traits, including optimism, may serve as buffers to childhood depression (Seligman, 2006). Effective treatment can help families strengthen these protective factors and minimize some of the risk factors.

Treatment

Several effective treatments are available for childhood depression. Some of the most common include:

- Cognitive-behavioral therapy, which assists children to identify and modify the negative thoughts that often accompany depression;
- Interpersonal therapy, which is a brief and highly structured manualized treatment designed to treat depression by examining relationships and transitions and how they affect thoughts and feelings;
- Individual psychotherapy, which is tailored to particular children and may include social skills training as well as cognitive-behavioral and interpersonal interventions; and
- Antidepressant medication.

In addition, practitioners generally offer some form of family psychoeducation, which is designed to offer education about depression and its treatment, to strengthen coping skills, and to provide support for family members (see Fristad & Arnold, 2004). Other interventions, such as family therapy, may be appropriate for particular families, such as those with multiple problems. Individual and family interventions are usually the initial recommendations for mild or moderate depression. In combination with psychosocial interventions, antidepressants are often prescribed for children who have major depression, whose symptoms are severe and disabling, or who have not responded to psychosocial interventions. There is evidence that the combination of psychotherapy and antidepressants is more effective than medication alone for the treatment of major depression.

As in the treatment of anxiety disorders, the selective serotonin reuptake inhibitors (SSRIs) are the most commonly prescribed antidepressants, including Celexa, Lexapro, Luvox, Paxil, Prozac, and Zoloft. Other commonly prescribed antidepressants include Effexor, Desyrel, Remeron, Serzone, and Wellbutrin. Given the media attention to concerns about the increased risk of suicide associated with the use of SSRI antidepressants for children, families are likely to have questions—and reservations—about these medications. As noted in Chapter 7, in 2004 the Food and Drug Administration (FDA) issued a public warning about an increased risk of suicidal thoughts or behavior in children and adolescents treated with SSRI medications and adopted a "black box" warning indicating the risk. In 2008, however, the National Institute of Mental Health reported results of a comprehensive review of pediatric trials conducted between 1988 and 2006 that suggested the benefits of antidepressant medications likely outweigh their risks to children and adolescents with depression. In the FDA review, no completed suicides occurred in children treated with SSRI medications, although about 4% experienced suicidal thinking or behavior, including actual suicide attempts (twice the rate of those taking placebos).

If antidepressants are prescribed for children with major depression, practitioners should share these research findings with parents in a discussion of the potential risks and benefits of medication, as well as the risks of no psychopharmacological treatment. If a course of medication is undertaken, young patients should be carefully monitored for side effects and complications, including the possible presence of suicidal ideation and behavior. Additional medications, including antipsychotics, may be prescribed when other symptoms are present, such as the hallucinations and delusions that may occur in major depression. Electroconvulsive therapy may be helpful for depressed adolescents who have not responded to other treatments (Fristad, Shaver, & Holderle, 2002).

Preventing Suicide

Suicide is one of the leading causes of death among young people and a major public health problem that is often preventable. According to the Centers for Disease Control and Prevention (2007; http://www.cdc.gov/injury/), about 2 million teenagers attempt suicide every year. In 2005, 16.9% of high school students reported that they had seriously considered attempting suicide during the past year; more than 8% of students reported that they had actually attempted suicide one or more times during that period. Suicides are closely linked to serious mental illness, including untreated major depression, bipolar disorder, and schizophrenia. Thus, when working with families of children with any of these disorders, clinicians need to discuss the material in this section.

The American Association of Suicidology (2007; http://www .suicidology.org/) provides much information about suicide, including child and adolescent suicide. The Web site notes that

- Many suicides are preventable.
- Most suicidal people desperately want to live, but are unable to see alternatives to their problems.
- Most suicidal people give definite warnings of their intentions.
- Talking about suicide does not cause someone to become suicidal.
- Major depression is the psychiatric diagnosis most often associated with completed suicide.
- Lifetime risk among untreated patients with major depression is nearly 20%.
- About two-thirds of people who complete suicide are depressed at the time of their death.
- Risk of suicide in people with major depression is about 20 times that of the general population.
- Treatments are effective 60% to 80% of the time.

Given the link between major depression and suicide, clinicians should talk with families about the risk factors and warning signs of suicide, as well as possible interventions. Many lists of risk factors and warning signs are available, such as those on the Web sites of the Centers for Disease Control and Prevention (2007; http://www.cdc.gov/ injury/) and the American Academy of Child & Adolescent Psychiatry (2007; http://www.aacap.org/). These include:

- Family history of suicide or violence;
- Family history of child maltreatment;
- Previous suicide attempt;
- History of depression or other mental illness;

- History of alcohol or drug abuse;
- Feelings of hopelessness;
- Impulsive or aggressive tendencies;
- Cultural or religious beliefs that suicide is a noble resolution of a personal dilemma;
- Local epidemic of suicide;
- Isolation or a feeling of being cut off from other people;
- Barriers to accessing mental health treatment;
- Early or current loss, such as the death of a parent;
- Physical illness;
- Easy access to lethal methods;
- Change in eating or sleeping habits;
- Withdrawal from friends, family, and regular activities;
- Violent actions, rebellious behavior, or running away;
- Marked personality change;
- Persistent boredom, difficulty concentrating, or a decline in academic performance;
- Frequent complaints about physical symptoms, such as stomachaches, headaches, or fatigue;
- Loss of interest in pleasurable activities;
- Complaints of being a bad person or feeling terrible inside;
- Suicidal statements, such as "I want to kill myself"; and
- Putting affairs in order, such as giving away favorite possessions or throwing away important belongings.

If there is a risk of suicide, practitioners may incorporate a suicide prevention contract into the treatment plan (see Barnard, 2003). They should also discuss potential responses with families. Many resources offer suggestions for parents, including the work of Fristad and Arnold (2004) and Oster and Montgomery (1995), the American Academy of Child & Adolescent Psychiatry (http://www.aacap.org/), and the Massachusetts General Hospital School Psychiatry Program & MADI Resource Center (http://www.massgeneral.org/schoolpsychiatry/). It is important for parents to:

- Always take suicidal talk seriously and immediately seek professional assistance.
- Recognize that suicidal talk is either an indication of intent to act or a cry for help—in both cases, attention is needed.
- Demonstrate your support.
- Ask the adolescent about depression or suicidal thoughts, which provides reassurance that someone cares and an opportunity to talk about problems.
- Increase supervision—do not leave a suicidal adolescent alone.
- Remove all potentially dangerous items, such as weapons, pills, or alcohol, from the home.
- Identify appropriate methods for expressing feelings of hopelessness or self-destruction, such as painting or music.
- Develop and implement a crisis plan, such as providing an around-the-clock watch and a written agreement stating that the teenager will not attempt suicide during a specified time period.
- Know how and when to access the emergency room and hospitalization.
- Discuss your concerns with your child's treatment team.
- Help the adolescent examine the impact of suicidal behavior on others.
- Establish a hierarchy of people for the student to contact in school if he or she has suicidal thoughts.

Fristad and Arnold (2004) recommended that families develop a crisis information file that includes (a) emergency phone numbers, such as family or friends who can offer assistance, the prescribing physician, and the therapist; (b) medication information, such as a complete listing of medication names, dosages, and times administered, as well as fact sheets that describe side effects and how to handle them; and (c) hospitalization information, such as address, directions, and insurance coverage. Clinicians may also want to talk with parents about what not to do, including being sworn to secrecy (suicidal teenagers need help), leaving a suicidal child or adolescent alone, trying to be a therapist, or pointing out that other people have worse problems.

Helping Families Cope With Depression

Several useful resources are available for families, including books for parents and for young people themselves. Books for parents include *Adolescent Depression* (Mondimore, 2002); *Helping Your Depressed Child* (Barnard, 2003); *Helping Your Depressed Teenager* (Oster & Montgomery, 1995); and *Raising a Moody Child: How to Cope With Depression and Bipolar Disorder* (Fristad & Arnold, 2004).

A helpful resource for teenagers is *Recovering From Depression: A Workbook for Teens* (Copeland & Copans, 2002). This adolescent workbook covers learning about depression, using strategies for feeling better, maintaining a positive outlook, and building an ongoing recovery and safety plan. Another book for teens, *When Nothing Matters Anymore: A Survival Guide for Depressed Teens* (Cobain, 2007), provides useful information about depression, getting help, and staying well. In addition, self-help books written for adults may be adapted for use with younger patients, including *Beating Depression: The Journey to Hope* (Jackson-Triche, Wells, & Minnium, 2002) and *The Depression Workbook: A Guide for Living With Depression and Manic Depression* (Copeland, 2001).

Parents may also benefit from reading personal accounts of people who have learned how to survive major depression and to construct fulfilling lives. Describing his own depression in *Darkness Visible: A Memoir of Madness*, for example, Pulitzer Prize-winning author William Styron (1990) wrote of enduring "the despair beyond despair" yet returning from "the abyss" with his capacity for joy and serenity restored.

Helping Children Cope With Depression at Home

There are many ways in which families can offer assistance and support at home, including the general strategies mentioned in Chapter 6, as well as some coping strategies suggested for dealing with anxiety disorders in Chapter 7. Both depressed and anxious children can benefit when parents adjust expectations until symptoms improve, teach relaxation techniques, encourage the use of self-calming strategies, assist the child to identify and counter negative thoughts, and encourage positive self-talk. Often, the best approach is simply to ask, "What can I do to help?" Children and adolescents can usually let parents know what is most helpful—a hug or a movie or simply a presence.

Parents also need to take care of themselves. Living with someone who is depressed is a depressing experience. Family members sometimes need to be reminded not to take illness-related symptoms personally. They need to seek support for themselves as well as professional assistance for personal or family problems. As discussed, family members can benefit from good communication, stress management, problem-solving, and assertiveness skills. Parents also need to prevent the depression from taking over their lives and to make time for themselves, their spouse or partner, and their well children. As always, it is essential for families to maintain a hopeful attitude, which is both appropriate and life affirming for the entire family. With effective treatment, most young people with depression recover, remain well for long periods of time, and lead productive and reasonably normal lives.

Based on the publications mentioned in the section on helping families cope as well as other resources, such as the Massachusetts General Hospital School Psychiatry Program and MADI Resource Center (http://www.massgeneral.org/schoolpsychiatry/), we offer families suggestions that are specifically focused on depression. Clinicians can assist parents to:

- Learn about depression, its symptoms, and its treatment;
- Understand the role of medication in treatment;
- Help prevent relapse by ensuring that a child takes medicine as prescribed;
- Distinguish between the child and the depressive illness (e.g., "it's the illness talking");
- Place childhood depression in perspective, as only one aspect of their family;

- Simplify home life to avoid a busy afterschool schedule or a long list of household chores, which may add to the child's sense of feeling burdened;
- Acknowledge and reinforce small steps;
- Post affirming photographs, posters, or aphorisms in the child's room;
- Recognize that children with major depression often struggle heroically simply to get through the day—or even to get out of bed;
- Respond immediately and appropriately when the child is faced with upsetting events; and
- Develop a crisis plan that specifies what actions are to be taken and by whom (see Copeland & Copans, 2002).

Therapists can also assist parents to work directly with their child. For example, parents can help young patients to:

- Maintain their perspective by recognizing the positive things in their lives;
- Identify their positive qualities;
- Live one day at a time and remember that depression passes;
- Focus on the future, including educational and career plans;
- Monitor their moods and symptoms;
- Recognize personal triggers of depressive symptoms, such as being overtired, bored, overstimulated, or isolated;
- Recognize interpersonal triggers of depression, such as being teased or feeling left out or rejected;
- Recognize and respond to early warning signs of depression, such as increased anxiety or irritability, withdrawal, or altered eating or sleeping patterns;
- If early warning signs are present, contact the therapist or reach out to trusted adults;
- Communicate openly with the therapist;
- Participate in developing a safety or crisis plan;
- Maintain a healthy lifestyle that includes proper nutrition, sufficient sleep, and moderate exercise;

- Avoid alcohol and recreational drugs, which can increase the risk of depressive symptoms and suicide;
- Schedule pleasurable activities, such as biking or taking the dog for a walk, that can counteract depression;
- Engage in creative activities, such as journaling or painting, as a means of expressing depressed feelings;
- Expand their support network, including peers, extended family members, and caring others;
- Develop social skills that enhance peer relations; and
- Assist others by volunteering at a church, school, hospital, or other community group.

Helping Children Cope With Depression in School

As we mentioned, students with depressive disorders should be encouraged to function as normally as possible in a regular classroom. As Fristad and Arnold (2004) discussed, however, the core symptoms of depression, including mood changes, loss of interest, fatigue, poor concentration, and psychomotor agitation or retardation, as well as the medication regimen or side effects, can have a major impact in school. They listed some possible accommodations for problems related to mood disorders:

- Difficulty concentrating: Provide a quiet place to work, allow for headphones with quiet music.
- Social withdrawal or excessive peer conflict: Provide extra support from a teacher during recess and lunch, arrange "special time" with another staff person.
- Difficulty staying focused during unstructured times: Increase structure, develop a buddy system if feasible.
- Daily mood changes: Present the most challenging activities during periods of most positive mood, increase teacher awareness of mood changes.

- Frequent urination due to medication: Give permission for the student to use the bathroom more frequently.
- Fluctuations in energy level: Plan energizing activities for periods of fatigue, plan a daily rest period, design daily activity schedules to match the student's typical activity level changes.

Many of the school-based interventions discussed in Chapter 6 can be adapted for students with depression. Given the fatigue and loss of energy that often accompany depression, it may be helpful for school personnel to monitor the student's moods on a daily basis to determine which activities can be undertaken successfully, to accommodate late arrival due to difficulty awakening, to begin the day with less-demanding academic tasks, to break the class into smaller time blocks, to allow the student specified "rest" periods during the day, to introduce physical activities periodically, and to modify academic assignments and evaluation procedures to reflect any illness-related limitations. Because students with depression often withdraw from peers and activities, they can be encouraged to participate in school-sponsored activities. In addition, if appropriate staff are available, cognitive-behavioral strategies may be used to counter feelings of hopelessness and helplessness and to modify negative or irrational thoughts.

Patrice Finley: The Treatment Plan

Returning to Patrice Finley and her family, Patrice has already received a diagnosis of major depression. As specified in the treatment plan, the long-term goals are to assist Patrice and her family to understand and accept her depressive disorder, to engage them in the treatment plan, to help them manage the symptoms of the disorder, and to support Patrice in achieving her personal objectives. Her individualized treatment plan might include the following interventions:

- Refer Patrice for a medication consult to determine is she is an appropriate candidate for antidepressant medication.
- Provide family psychoeducation for the Finley family to educate them about major depression and its treatment, to strengthen their coping skills, and to offer support.
- Provide cognitive-behavioral therapy to help Patrice identify and replace negative or irrational thoughts with more positive and realistic thoughts.
- Provide interpersonal therapy to explore the impact of relationships on her depression.
- Provide individual psychotherapy that assists Patrice to understand and resolve concerns that may trigger or exacerbate her depressive symptoms.
- Help Patrice and her family identify triggers and early warning signs of a depressive episode.
- Work with Patrice and her family to develop a crisis plan and a suicide prevention contract.
- Work with Patrice and her family to implement these strategies at home.
- Collaborate with the school in developing an Individualized Education Plan (IEP) that gives permission for more frequent bathroom use due to medication side effects, adjusts the homework load to prevent Patrice from feeling overwhelmed, allows extra time to complete certain types of assignments, permits her to take a time-out when a situation feels unmanageable, and offers a counselor-facilitated group of peers with similar problems.

The therapist can also work with the Finley family to develop a family service plan that can help them identify and prioritize their needs, deal with illness-related concerns, and make an informed choice about their use of other available services. For example, the family might request several sessions for the entire family, including Patrice's grandmother, to develop safety and crisis plans as well as periodic family sessions to address other issues as they arise.

Working With the Finley Family

Social worker Ron Cassidy is a staff member at a hospital-based mental health clinic. He works with the families of children and adolescents who receive services at the clinic and has already met with Jocelyn and Jamal Finley to obtain a history during the evaluation of Patrice.

Ron: Mr. and Mrs. Finley, it's good to see you again. As I told you when we meet earlier, as soon as we finished our evaluation, I would meet with you again to share our results and recommendations. Patrice has already met with our psychiatrist and psychologist. I'm sure it has been very difficult for you to see these changes in your daughter.

Jocelyn: Mr. Cassidy, it has been devastating! I've never felt so hopeless and helpless in my life. Watching Patrice change from a happy child and an excellent student to someone who doesn't seem to care about anything—including herself—has been so difficult. I've been crying a lot myself. It feels as if I've lost the daughter I knew so well. Even our other children, Jerome and Edward, have been affected. And so has my mother, Sharise, who lives with us and is very close to Patrice.

Ron: Please call me Ron. When someone develops a mental illness such as depression, it does affect the entire family. That's why we work so closely with families. We want to develop plans to assist Patrice, but we also want to meet the needs of your family.

Jamal: But can Patrice be helped? She just seems to get more and more depressed and spends most of her time alone in her room.

Ron: The changes you've seen in Patrice are symptoms of major depression, which is the most severe form of depression. Teenagers with major depression are typically unhappy and have little interest in friends or activities. They may have trouble sleeping, have little energy, feel worthless, and believe their life is not worth living. As you know, Patrice sometimes thinks of suicide and is in considerable distress. Often, these adolescents have difficulty concentrating, and their grades are affected.

Jocelyn: But what can we do to help her?

Ron: Fortunately, we have effective treatments for depression. Because of the severity of Patrice's depression, we are recommending an antidepressant medication, which should reduce the intensity of her symptoms. There is much evidence that antidepressants help a majority of those with major depression. I have some materials that provide information about the medication, as well as its potential benefits and risks. A small number of young patients on these medications may actually have increased thoughts of suicide, so we need to work closely with you and with Patrice to see how she responds. But, the benefits of antidepressants outweigh the risks, especially when the depression is severe and persistent.

Jamal: I hate to see her on drugs. Aren't there any other treatments?

Ron: In milder cases of depression, we often try other treatments initially to see if medication is needed. In Patrice's case, our psychiatrist is concerned about her level of distress, as well as the risk of suicide, as I know you are. We want to give her some relief as soon as possible. Once you have read the materials, we'll answer any questions you have. If you decide to follow our recommendation for medication, we'll work with you to monitor its effectiveness. If the medication is not effective or there are unacceptable side effects, we have several other antidepressants we can use, but we never recommend using medication alone.

Jocelyn: What else are you recommending?

Ron: We are recommending several other treatments that are effective for major depression, although we'll need to see what works best for Patrice. We are recommending cognitive-behavioral therapy to help Patrice identify and replace negative or irrational thoughts, such as her feelings of worthlessness and guilt, with more positive and realistic thoughts. In addition, we're recommending individual psychotherapy to help Patrice understand and resolve her concerns and to help her improve her relationships, which are often important in depression. We would also like to work with all of you to identify triggers and early warning signs of depression, which can help Patrice reduce the risk of relapse and hospitalization. Here are some materials that describe these treatments and present research support for their effectiveness. Patrice is very eager to learn how to manage her depressive symptoms, and we feel she is an excellent candidate for these treatments.

Jocelyn: What about the risk of suicide? That's our major concern right now.

Ron: That's our concern as well, so we want to meet as soon as possible with you and Patrice to develop a crisis plan and a suicide prevention contract.

Jocelyn: What about the rest of our family—my mother, Sharise, and our other children, Jerome and Edward.

Ron: We prefer to work with the entire family whenever possible so that all of you can play a role in helping Patrice. Let's schedule a family session. Then, we can meet in the future as often as needed.

Jamal: What about her grades? She always received As and Bs in the past, but now she's in danger of failing.

Ron: I realize Patrice's major depression has significantly affected her ability to function in school. With your permission, we can share results of our evaluation with the school so they can determine if Patrice is eligible for special education services.

Jocelyn: We'd really appreciate your help with the school. I know very little about special education.

Ron: Is there anything else I can do for you today?

Jamal: I don't think so. We need to go over the materials you gave us on medication and the other treatments. But your recommendations make sense to me. We want to do all we can to help Patrice.

Ron: I know you do. You've already been very helpful to Patrice, and she feels very lucky to have your love and support. I look forward to working with you.

CHAPTER NINE

Talking to Families About Bipolar Disorder

Jennifer McCone was a difficult child from birth. As an infant, she resisted a regular schedule and experienced persistent bouts of colic. Although she progressed normally during her preschool years, Jennifer periodically erupted in intense, prolonged temper tantrums that left her—and her parents—exhausted. In elementary school, she did well academically, but several of her teachers commented on the severe emotional outbursts that occurred when she was frustrated or tired. Although her parents, Elizabeth and David, were concerned, Jennifer was usually a sweet and loving child who was popular with her peers and cherished by her family. Everyone assumed that she was simply being herself. At the onset of adolescence, however, Jennifer began to manifest more serious problems, including severe mood swings. Occasionally, she was unusually happy or silly; at other times, she was very irritable, angry, and agitated; and at still other times, she was depressed and spoke of death and suicide. Sometimes, Jennifer seemed to have limitless energy and went without sleep for a day or more, followed by periods when she complained of fatigue, poor concentration, and boredom. After a particularly difficult period, her pediatrician referred the family to the local mental health center, where Jennifer was hospitalized and diagnosed with bipolar disorder. Reeling from their daughter's deterioration and hospitalization, the McCones wondered what Jennifer's mental illness would mean for her future and for their family.

The Substance Abuse and Mental Health Services Administration (2005; SAMHSA; http://mentalhealth.samhsa.gov/) estimates that bipolar disorder affects at least 750,000 children in the United States. Bipolar disorder is often difficult to recognize and diagnose in children, however, and the diagnosis raises many questions. For example, the National Institute of Mental Health (NIMH, 2007) has reported a 40-fold increase in the rate of diagnosing bipolar disorder among youth in the past decade. It is unclear what is causing this increase, but current evidence suggestions a combination of factors, including the underdiagnosis of bipolar disorder in the past, the overdiagnosis of the disorder in the present, and an increase of childhood behavioral disorders.

The NIMH report noted that one problem is the use of the *Diagnostic and Statistical Manual of Mental Disorders, Fourth Edition, Text Revision* (*DSM-IV-TR*; American Psychiatric Association, 2000) diagnostic criteria for children. Researchers have found that some children clearly meet the diagnostic criteria for bipolar disorder, but a much larger group shows some but not all of the symptoms. This latter group frequently manifests excessive irritability and impulsivity, but it is not clear that these symptoms are indicative of bipolar disorder. It is also unclear that all of the children currently diagnosed with bipolar disorder will grow up to be adults with the disorder. Because only a small fraction of children actually meet the criteria for bipolar disorder, as the NIMH report indicated, it seems likely that many of these young people do not have the same illness as adults.

In spite of these areas of disagreement, there is considerable evidence supporting the validity of the bipolar diagnosis in children and adolescents (Youngstrom, Birmaher, & Findling, 2008). Furthermore, from a clinical perspective, whatever the unresolved questions regarding the overdiagnosis or misdiagnosis of bipolar disorder, these children and their families experience significant distress. Thus, practitioners face substantial challenges in working with this diverse group of children and families.

Following a specification of the diagnostic criteria for bipolar disorder, we discuss risk factors, treatment, and coping strategies for home and school. We then return to Jennifer McCone and her family, suggest some possible interventions, and offer an illustrative session with her parents.

Diagnostic Criteria for Bipolar Disorder

Along with depression, bipolar disorder is characterized by a disturbance in mood. There are actually three types of bipolar disorder—sometimes called the *bipolar spectrum* (Akiskal, 2008)—which vary in severity, chronicity, and persistence: bipolar I disorder, bipolar II disorder, and cyclothymia.

Bipolar I disorder is characterized by one or more manic or mixed episodes. A *manic episode* is a distinct period of abnormally and persistently elevated, expansive, or irritable mood. The following symptoms may be present: inflated self-esteem or grandiosity, decreased need for sleep, increased talkativeness or pressured speech, flight of ideas or racing thoughts, distractibility, increase in goal-directed activity or psychomotor agitation, and excessive involvement in pleasurable activities that have a high potential for negative consequences, such as buying sprees or sexual indiscretions. During a *mixed episode*, the criteria are met for both manic and major depressive episodes. The mood disturbance is sufficiently severe to cause marked functional impairment, may necessitate hospitalization, and may include psychotic features, such as hallucinations and delusions.

Bipolar II disorder is characterized by one or more major depressive episodes accompanied by at least one hypomanic episode. A *hypomanic episode* is marked by symptoms that are similar to those of a manic episode and is associated with an observable change in functioning. The episode is not severe enough to cause marked functional impairment or to necessitate hospitalization, however, and there are no psychotic features. A diagnosis of bipolar disorder not otherwise specified is sometimes used for children and adolescents whose symptoms do not meet the full *DSM-IV-TR* diagnostic criteria for bipolar disorder.

Cyclothymic disorder is characterized by numerous periods of hypomanic symptoms that do not meet the criteria for a manic episode and numerous periods of depressive symptoms that do not meet the criteria for a major depressive episode. The individual has not been without symptoms for more than 2 months at a time during a specified period of time (2 years for adults, 1 year for children). The symptoms cause clinically significant distress or functional impairment.

When major depressive episodes are present, both bipolar disorder I and II may manifest a seasonal pattern, during which the episodes begin during a particular season, most often in fall or winter. Likewise, both bipolar disorders may be characterized by rapid cycling, which is the occurrence of four or more mood episodes during the past year. For all types of bipolar disorder, it is essential to determine whether the symptoms are due to another condition, such as substance abuse, medication, or a medical condition. In addition, maniclike episodes may be triggered by antidepressant treatment and should not count toward a diagnosis of bipolar disorder.

Risk Factors

There is strong evidence for the role of biological factors in bipolar disorder (see Miklowitz, 2002; Torrey & Knable, 2002), although the etiological picture is complex. Important biological factors include:

- Genetic factors, with strong evidence from family, adoption, and twin studies that close relatives of people with bipolar disorder are at increased risk for developing the disorder;
- Neurochemical factors, such as neurotransmitter abnormalities; and
- Other biological factors, such as limbic, endocrine, and immune dysfunction.

Although most experts doubt that environmental factors alone can cause bipolar disorder without the contributing influences and genetics and other biological factors, there is strong evidence that high levels of stress can affect the course of the disorder and increase the risk of an episode (Miklowitz, 2002). This vulnerability–stress model accounts for many research findings and offers a blueprint for treatment as well as for home- and school-based interventions.

Based on their review of adult outcome studies of bipolar disorder, Torrey and Knable (2002) estimated that 25% of people recover completely, 55% to 65% recovery partially, and 10% to 20% have continuing symptoms with a poor outcome. Predictors of outcome include positive prognostic signs, such as adherence to the medication regime, and negative prognostic signs, such as the presence of delusions, prominent rapid cycling and mixed states, and a diagnosis of schizoaffective disorder, which meets the diagnostic criteria of a mood disorder and schizophrenia.

Treatment

Although most of the research has been conducted with adults who have bipolar disorder (see Miklowitz & Otto, 2008), the following treatments are also used to treat childhood bipolar disorder:

- Cognitive-behavioral therapy, which assists older children and adolescents to identify and modify maladaptive thoughts that can accompany bipolar disorder;

- Interpersonal and social rhythm therapy, which assists them to maintain a regular schedule of daily activities and stability in personal relationships;
- Individual psychotherapy, which is tailored to particular young patients and may help them understand and accept the illness, enhance their coping skills, and improve their self-esteem and relationships; and
- Mood stabilizers, which are designed to control current symptoms and to reduce the frequency and severity of future episodes.

In addition, treatment for child and adolescent bipolar disorder generally includes family psychoeducation, which is designed to offer education about bipolar disorder and its treatment, to strengthen coping skills, and to support family members. This intervention is an evidence-based treatment for adults with bipolar disorder, and there is also evidence of its effectiveness with young patients (Fristad & Arnold, 2004).

Mood stabilizers are often prescribed for children with bipolar disorder, including lithium, anticonvulsants such as Tegretol or Depakote, and new anticonvulsant mood stabilizers. There is strong support for the effectiveness of mood stabilizers in treating bipolar disorder, including some studies with children and adolescents. Although additional controlled studies are needed with young patients, the available findings are promising (Fristad et al., 2002). Sometimes, multiple medications are prescribed to target different symptoms. For example, both mood stabilizers and antidepressants may be prescribed to control the manic and depressive episodes of bipolar disorder, respectively. Likewise, antipsychotic medication may be prescribed if hallucinations and delusions are present. As in the case of major depression, electroconvulsive therapy may be prescribed for certain patients, such as those who have not responded to other interventions, although data are sparse regarding its efficacy for children and adolescents with bipolar disorder (Fristad et al., 2002).

Fristad and Arnold (2004) provided an excellent discussion of the role of medication in treating child and adolescent mood disorders.

They reported that there is some evidence for the safety and efficacy of mood stabilizers with young patients, although most research has been conducted with adults and some of these medications have not been approved for use with children. On the other hand, untreated bipolar disorder has a devastating impact on children and families. Clinicians can assist families to consider the possible risks and benefits of medication, and of no medication, and to make an informed decision about its use. Families should be aware that psychopharmacology is as much an art as a science, that partial responses to new medications are common, and that it may take time to find an effective medication and dose. Medication is never the sole treatment for children and adolescents. Psychosocial interventions can assist children and families to understand and cope with bipolar disorder, to reduce the risk of future episodes, and to enhance the quality of their lives.

Some unique issues arise in professional practice with patients who have bipolar disorder. People with mental illness typically welcome treatments that can eliminate or reduce their anxiety or depressive or psychotic symptoms. In contrast, many individuals with bipolar disorder are reluctant to give up their high periods, which are often accompanied by euphoria, grandiosity, excitement, and drama. In her personal account of life with bipolar disorder, *An Unquiet Mind: A Memoir of Moods and Madness*, psychologist Kay Redfield Jamison (1995) wrote that she finally took medication only because the alternatives were death and insanity. Once she was stabilized on lithium, however, she greatly missed the intensity and exhilaration of her moods:

I had a horrible sense of loss for who I had been and where I had been. It was difficult to give up the high flights of mind and mood, even though the depressions that inevitably followed nearly cost me my life. My family and friends expected that I would welcome being "normal," be appreciative of lithium, and take in stride having normal energy and sleep. But if you have had stars at your feet and the rings of planets through your hands, are used to sleeping only four or five hours a night and now sleep eight, are used to staying up all night for days and weeks in a row and now cannot, it is a very real adjustment to blend into a three-piece-suit schedule, which, while comfortable to many, is new, restrictive, seemingly less productive, and maddeningly less in-toxicating. . . . When I am my present "normal" self, I am far re-moved from when I have been my liveliest, most productive, most intense, most outgoing and effervescent. (pp. 91–92)

Like many patients with bipolar disorder, Jamison, an expert on mood disorders, was reluctant to take her medication for many years after her initial diagnosis. Thus, clinicians should be sensitive to this poten-tial resistance to medication among adolescents, who tend to see them-selves as invulnerable and often welcome the exuberance of mania.

In addition, as Jamison (1996) discussed in *Touched With Fire: Manic-Depressive Illness and the Artistic Temperament*, several stud-ies have documented an association between bipolar disorder and creativity among writers, visual artists, and musicians. As Jamison ob-served, mania offers certain advantages to creative people, such as heightened imaginative powers; intensified emotional responses; in-creased energy; increased fluency, rapidity, and flexibility; and altered perception, which allows them to see things in original ways. The depressive phase increases their awareness of terror and anguish, puts them in touch with human suffering, and motivates them to channel their painful emotions into creative activities.

Thus, there has been some reluctance among creative individuals with bipolar disorder to follow the medication regime for fear that they will lose their muse. Resisting or stopping medication is associ-ated with a high risk of recurrence, however, as well as an increased risk of suicide (Miklowitz, 2002). As Jamison (1995) pointed out, un-treated bipolar disorder is destructive, often psychotic, and sometimes lethal.

Helping Families Cope With Bipolar Disorder

Because depression is typically present in bipolar disorder, both Chapter 8 and 9 should inform professional practice with families of children and adolescents who have bipolar disorder. In this chapter, we focus specifically on bipolar disorder, but all of the resources and coping strategies for childhood depression are relevant to bipolar disorder. In fact, some of the best resources address both mood disorders.

Two excellent books for parents are *The Bipolar Teen: What You Can Do to Help Your Child and Your Family* (Miklowitz & George, 2008) and *Raising a Moody Child: How to Cope With Depression and Bipolar Disorder* (Fristad & Arnold, 2004). Other books for parents include *The Bipolar Child* (Papolos & Papolos, 2006); *Bipolar Kids: Helping Your Child Find Calm in the Mood Storm* (R. Greenberg, 2007); *Parenting a Bipolar Child* (Faedda & Austin, 2006); *Understanding the Mind of Your Bipolar Child* (Lombardo, 2006); and *The Ups and Downs of Raising a Bipolar Child: A Survival Guide for Parents* (Lederman & Fink, 2003). These authors provide information about getting an accurate diagnosis, finding the right treatment, managing mood swings, distinguishing between the disorder and the child, and solving problems at home and in school.

Books for children and adolescents themselves include those mentioned in Chapter 8 on depression, as well as *My Bipolar, Roller Coaster, Feelings Book* (Herbert, 2005). There are also some excellent books on adult bipolar disorder, including *The Bipolar Disorder Survival Guide* (Miklowitz, 2002); *The Depression Workbook: A Guide for Living With Depression and Manic Depression* (Copeland, 2001); and *Surviving Manic Depression* (Torrey & Knable, 2002). These adult-oriented books have much useful information and provide many coping strategies that can be adapted to young people with bipolar disorder. Parents and adolescents may also benefit from reading personal accounts of people with bipolar disorder, such as Jamison's (1995) memoir, which portrays her journey with power and eloquence, and *Hurry Down Sunshine,* Michael Greenberg's (2008) anguished personal account of his daughter's bipolar disorder.

Helping Children Cope With Bipolar Disorder at Home

Many of the suggestions offered in previous chapters are also appropriate for bipolar disorder. For example, it is helpful for parents to become well informed about bipolar disorder and its treatment, to maintain a supportive home environment, to respond appropriately to symptoms, to adjust expectations until symptoms improve, to encourage self-calming and anxiety management techniques, to identify and counter maladaptive thoughts, and to encourage positive self-talk. Clinicians can review those suggestions along with the strategies mentioned in this section, which focus specifically on bipolar disorder.

Miklowitz and George (2008) described the PEACE approach to coping with bipolar disorder. The approach is based on five principles for maintaining good family relationships: (a) problem solving; (b) education about the disorder; (c) acceptance of the disorder and its limitations; (d) communication skills; and (e) escape from the situation when necessary, such as by exiting from unproductive interactions.

Fristad and Arnold (2004) mentioned some things that parents of children and adolescents with bipolar disorder should avoid:

- Reassuring the child too rapidly that everything is fine;
- Taking comments literally or personally when a child is experiencing a manic or hypomanic episode;
- Attempting to be constantly available and positive—parents are human, too;
- Feeling guilty for the child's problems or for not meeting every need;
- Allowing the disorder to take over family life, such as avoiding family outings for fear of an incident occurring; and

• Making big decisions during an episode, such as about divorce, custody, or job changes.

In contrast, based on the publications mentioned in the preceding section, as well as other resources, there are many strategies that can assist families to cope with bipolar disorder at home. Some of these strategies focus on the home environment. For example, clinicians can help parents:

• Establish a stable, low-stress, consistent, and predictable home environment;
• Strive for a balance between supportive flexibility and appropriate limit setting;
• Avoid under- or overregulation with too few or too many household rules;
• Maintain a structured daily schedule that consists of times and activities, such as a time for awakening, for being dressed for breakfast, for completing homework, for enjoying free time, and for bedtime;
• Focus on short-term goals and reinforce success and effort;
• Keep the "small stuff" small by choosing those issues worth having an argument over and those that are not;
• Take a time-out when their efforts do not seem to be helping;
• Limit the child's viewing of stimulating videos and television shows;
• Plan in advance for transitions, such as a new home or school, which are often difficult for children with bipolar disorder;
• Recognize that holidays are often overstimulating for children with bipolar disorder and may trigger mood changes; and
• During hectic periods, help the child cope by using a quiet zone, some outdoor time, and video or other games.

The symptoms of bipolar disorder are often challenging for parents, who can benefit from professional assistance in responding appropriately. For instance, it is generally helpful for parents to:

- Remain calm when the child is heading into a manic episode;
- Recognize and respond to the early warning signs of mania, such as changes in activity and energy levels, in thinking and perception, in sleep patterns, or in behavior;
- "Put on the brakes" when manic symptoms develop by encouraging children to limit activities;
- Avoid arguing when children manifest symptomatic behavior, such as grandiosity or inflated self-esteem;
- Be matter-of-fact in responding to unacceptable behavior, such as sexually inappropriate behavior, or to outrageous demands;
- Try to distract the child by engaging in activities if time alone in a quiet room does not seem to help;
- Consider possible reasons, such as medication change, medical illness, hormonal or other developmental changes, sleep, school, social life, seasonal factors, and substance use, when symptoms break through;
- Revisit the episode and discuss coping strategies that might have helped after a mood has passed and if the child seems receptive;
- Ensure that medications are being taken as prescribed;
- Prepare for a hospitalization if the child is at imminent risk of harm to self or others; or
- Develop a crisis plan that specifies what actions are to be taken and by whom (see Copeland & Copans, 2002).

Working with older children and adolescents, parents can assist them to understand and manage bipolar disorder. They can encourage their child to:

- Learn about bipolar disorder, its symptoms, and its treatment;
- Gradually assume more responsibility for managing the disorder;
- Maintain an optimal level of stimulation, which may vary from day to day;
- Keep a daily mood chart or social rhythm chart (see Lederman & Fink, 2003; Miklowitz, 2002; Miklowitz & George, 2008);

- Manage moods by learning to identify different mood states and to assign emotions to different levels of intensity;
- Use relaxation strategies, such as breathing exercises, visualization, muscle relaxation, or counting, to diffuse intense emotions;
- Encourage productive expression of moods, such as creative, physical, social, and leisure activities;
- Avoid disruptions of biological rhythms, such as sleep deprivation, which can induce manic episodes;
- Identify and avoid possible triggers of manic episodes, such as fatigue, hunger, overstimulation, and caffeine;
- Avoid alcohol and recreational drugs, which can exacerbate bipolar symptoms;
- Develop and maintain social supports;
- Recognize and inhibit the expression of negative emotions; and
- Recognize the consequences of out-of-control emotions, such as problems with parents or peers.

Helping Children Cope With Bipolar Disorder in School

Although students with bipolar disorder should be encouraged to function as normally as possible in a regular classroom, as Faedda and Austin (2006) pointed out, the symptoms of bipolar disorder include many shifts of mood, energy, motivation, and concentration that affect the ability to learn. They noted that the choice of school accommodations depends on many factors, including individual needs and circumstances, the stage of the illness, the effect of bipolar disorder on school functioning, and school-related stress. Thus, for many students with bipolar disorder, educational staff need to anticipate and accommodate learning and cognitive difficulties, which may vary in severity from day to day.

In addition to the school-based interventions presented in other chapters, during symptomatic phases, school personnel can modify classroom activities to reflect the student's elevated or irritable mood, increased talkativeness, racing thoughts, or distractibility. These symp-toms can undermine the ability of students to undertake academic activities successfully, to respond appropriately in class, and to con-centrate during examinations. Accommodations may also be necessary for medication side effects or seasonal problems. If appropriate staff are available, cognitive-behavioral strategies may be beneficial in deal-ing with the symptoms of bipolar disorder, such as grandiosity or im-pulsive risk-taking behavior.

Jennifer McCone: The Treatment Plan

Returning to Jennifer McCone and her family, Jennifer has already re-ceived a diagnosis of bipolar I disorder. As specified in the treatment plan, the long-term goals are to assist Jennifer and her family to under-stand and accept her bipolar disorder, to engage them in the treatment plan, to help them manage the symptoms of the disorder, and to sup-port Jennifer in achieving her personal objectives. The individualized treatment plan might include the following interventions:

- Refer Jennifer for a medication consult to determine is she is an appropriate candidate for a mood stabilizer.
- Provide family psychoeducation for the McCone family to educate them about bipolar disorder and its treatment, to strengthen their coping skills, and to offer support.
- Provide interpersonal and social rhythm therapy to help Jennifer maintain a regular schedule of daily activities and stability in her relationships.
- Provide cognitive-behavioral therapy to help her identify and replace maladaptive thoughts that often accompany bipolar disorder.
- Provide individual psychotherapy to help her understand and accept the illness and to address her issues and concerns.
- Help Jennifer and her family identify early warning signs and triggers of manic episodes.

- Work with Jennifer and her family to implement these strategies at home and to develop relapse prevention and crisis plans.
- Collaborate with the school in developing an Individualized Education Plan (IEP) that accommodates Jennifer's late arrival due to medication-related problems in awakening, provides opportunities for extra time and a quiet place for taking tests, offers weekly sessions with a school counselor to help her deal with illness-related symptoms and concerns, provides home-based assistance following relapse or hospitalization, and limits her course load by extending the term through summer school.

In addition, following family assessment, the clinician can work with the McCone family to formulate a family service plan designed to help them identify and prioritize their needs, deal with illness-related concerns, and make an informed choice about their use of other available services. For example, the family might request a referral to the 12-week educational program offered by the local affiliate of the National Alliance on Mental Illness (NAMI), as-needed consultation for her parents, and individual therapy for her mother, who has experienced depression herself during Jennifer's illness.

Working With the McCone Family

Psychiatrist Veronica Chang has an independent practice in Jennifer McCone's community. She is also affiliated with a university hospital that offers a full range of mental health services, including an adolescent inpatient unit. During Jennifer's hospitalization, Dr. Chang conducted an evaluation of Jennifer and is now following up with Elizabeth and David McCone regarding her outpatient treatment.

Dr. Chang: Please come in, Mr. and Mrs. McCone. We met briefly at the hospital, when I told you Jennifer's diagnosis of bipolar disorder. Now, I want to discuss the results of my evaluation in more detail, as well as my recommendations for Jennifer's treatment. I also want to answer your questions and learn how I can assist your family. I always work closely with families and think of my practice as a partnership with the patient and family.

Elizabeth: At this point, we're feeling confused and overwhelmed. We have no idea what to do next.

Dr. Chang: That's why I wanted to meet with you as soon as Jennifer was released from the hospital. I want to work with you in developing a treatment plan that helps all of you live with this challenging illness. As you know, Jennifer's official diagnosis is bipolar disorder I, which is characterized by both manic and depressive episodes. A manic episode is a period of very elevated or irritable mood. Symptoms include grandiose thoughts, such as an exaggerated sense of importance or power, as well as decreased need for sleep, increased talkativeness, and racing thoughts. I sometimes think of a manic episode as a revved-up motor that seems to be out of control. Jennifer also experiences depressive episodes that are marked by feelings of sadness, hopelessness, and worthlessness. It's almost as if the body and mind need to crash after a manic episode.

Elizabeth: But, what caused Jennifer's bipolar disorder? Why did this happen to her?

Dr. Chang: There is agreement that bipolar disorder often involves a genetic predisposition to develop the disorder. You mentioned several close relatives with mood disorders, including Jennifer's grandmother. Bipolar disorder is associated with certain biological abnormalities, such as abnormal brain chemistry. But, we also know that environmental factors, such as stress, can influence the course of the disorder and increase the risk of an episode. Many experts view bipolar disorder in terms of the vulnerability–stress model, which assumes there is a biological vulnerability that interacts with events in the person's life. The model provides a foundation for treatment. We can usually control the biological abnormalities with medication, but we also need to help patients and family members gain the knowledge and skills they need to manage the illness.

Elizabeth: That makes sense. As you mentioned, mood disorders do tend to run in our family. I've always been a bit depressed myself, although I've never received treatment. But I've been much more depressed since Jennifer's problems became so severe.

Dr. Chang: I want to learn more about your depression and see how I can help. So, let's return to that later. But unless you have other questions, I'd like to share my recommendations for Jennifer's treatment.

David: To be honest, I've been almost as worried about my wife as about Jennifer. I haven't known how to help either of them.

Dr. Chang: That's why I wanted to meet with you. We'll all play a role in Jennifer's treatment. As you know, Jennifer began taking a mood stabilizer during her hospitalization. We've already discussed the medication and provided you with some written materials. Do you have any questions?

Elizabeth: I think we have learned enough about the medication, but we're not sure what we should be looking for.

Dr. Chang: Let's go over the potential risks and side effects as well as the expected changes in symptoms. I've developed a checklist for families, so you'll know what to look for.

David: That should be very helpful. What should we do if we notice something that concerns us?

Dr. Chang: You have my office number, and I'll give you my answering service so that I can be reached when I'm not in my office. I'll also give you the number at the hospital in case I'm out of town. So, you'll always be able to reach someone. In addition to the medication, I'm also recommending other treatments for Jennifer. These include interpersonal and social rhythm therapy to help Jennifer maintain a regular schedule of daily activities and stability in her relationships, cognitive-behavioral therapy to help her identify and replace maladaptive thoughts that often accompany bipolar disorder, and individual psychotherapy to help her understand and accept the illness and to address her issues and concerns. I plan to meet with Jennifer on a weekly basis. I developed a few handouts that describe each of these treatments so that you are familiar with them. Once you've looked over the materials, I can answer your questions at our next meeting. I also want to meet with both of you and Jennifer to help you identify the early warning signs and triggers of her manic episodes so that we can reduce the frequency and severity of her episodes.

David: What about the school? Is there any way they can help?

Dr. Chang: Students with bipolar disorder are often eligible for special education services. I will write a report that you can share with the school. I'll also work with you in developing possible school-based interventions that you can discuss with the school. I see the school as part of our team. We'll all be working to help Jennifer. Here is some material that describes the procedures for determining eligibility, as well as some services in school that Jennifer may receive. There is also information about your rights as parents. After you've looked over the material, I can answer any questions. It will take some time to see how Jennifer responds to treatment. Once we see what works best, and perhaps what doesn't, we can make whatever changes are needed. Do you have any questions so far?

Elizabeth: No, you've explained things very well, although there seems to be so much to learn. At least I don't feel so helpless now that we're working with you.

Dr. Chang: Let's talk about the other services you may want. Mrs. McCone, I'd like to meet with you individually next week to see how I can help with your depression.

David: We'll be grateful for whatever assistance you can provide. My wife has been depressed for a long time, although it's never been this bad.

Elizabeth: What other services are available for our family?

Dr. Chang: You may be interested in a referral to the local chapter of the National Alliance on Mental Illness (NAMI), which offers a 12-week education program for family members, as well as an ongoing support group. The educational program provides information about mental illness, including bipolar disorder, and helps families develop the coping skills they need. Families generally find the program helpful.

Elizabeth: That sounds good. I think we would both benefit from the educational program. And, I've felt so alone in dealing with Jennifer's bipolar disorder. I'd appreciate the chance to talk with other parents in a support group.

CHAPTER TEN

Talking to Families
About Schizophrenia

*At the beginning of his senior year of high school, Anthony Pou-
los began behaving strangely. At first, his mother, Lynne, as-
cribed his increasingly erratic moods and lack of focus to the
stress the family had experienced in the past year. Her husband, Nicholas, had lost his job as an electrician due to a decline in construction locally, and the family barely managed
to cover their expenses with savings and Lynne's part-time employment as a secretary. During the same period, Nicholas's
mother, Eleni, came to live with them following the death of
her husband. The grandparents, who were close to Anthony
and his 14-year-old sister, Sophia, were first-generation Greek
immigrants, and Eleni spoke limited English. Nicholas had recently found employment, and the family began to feel more
secure about their future. But, Anthony continued to experience problems. When his grooming deteriorated and he began
to converse with himself, his pediatrician recommended that
Anthony be evaluated at the mental health unit of the local
hospital. During his evaluation, Anthony reported hearing
voices, claimed unnamed people were plotting against him,*

*and appeared frightened and confused. Following his evalua-
tion, the psychiatrist met briefly with his parents and informed
them that Anthony's diagnosis was paranoid schizophrenia.
No one had taken the time to explain the disorder or its treatment, and the entire family was in a state of shock. Was there
any hope for Anthony?*

Schizophrenia is a severe and persistent mental disorder that is characterized by a wide range of cognitive, social, behavioral, and emotional
symptoms. According to the National Institute of Mental Health (http://
www.nimh.nih.gov/), schizophrenia is relatively rare in children, affecting only about 1 in 40,000, compared to 1 in 100 adults. The onset
of schizophrenia is typically in late adolescence or early adulthood,
with an average age of onset of 18 in males and 25 in females. Thus,
like the family of Anthony Poulos, families may find themselves dealing
with one of the most challenging mental disorders just as their teenager is poised to cross the threshold to adulthood. Because of the rar-
ity of schizophrenia in childhood, in this chapter we focus largely on
adolescent schizophrenia.

Whatever the age of onset, schizophrenia has a devastating impact
on individuals and families. Indeed, the World Health Organization
(2001) has identified schizophrenia as one of the 10 most debilitating
diseases in developed countries worldwide. Individuals who have
schizophrenia suffer the terrors of psychosis, diminished life aspirations, and social devaluation. Media accounts of violence reinforce social stigma, although people with schizophrenia are more often victims
than perpetrators. Moreover, the expanding literature on the impact of
schizophrenia on families provides strong evidence that they share in
the tremendous losses and challenges that accompany the illness (e.g.,
Lefley, 1996; Marsh & Lefley, 2009). In response to the illness, as we
have discussed, families experience a subjective burden, which involves the emotional costs of coping with difficult behaviors and with
the pain and losses of a loved one, and an objective burden, which in-

volves the time, energy, and finances devoted to illness management. This burden is especially onerous in the case of schizophrenia.

Initially, we discuss the diagnostic criteria for schizophrenia as well as the subtypes of the disorder. Additional topics include risk factors for schizophrenia, treatment, and coping strategies for home and school. Finally, we return to Anthony Poulos and his family and offer some possible interventions as well as an illustrative session with his parents.

Diagnostic Criteria for Schizophrenia

The *Diagnostic and Statistical Manual of Mental Disorders, Fourth Edition, Text Revision* (*DSM-IV-TR*; American Psychiatric Association, 2000) diagnostic criteria for schizophrenia, which are the same for individuals of all ages, are categorized as positive and negative symptoms, and described in the section, "Schizophrenia and Other Psychotic Disorders." Positive symptoms appear to reflect an excess or distortion of normal functions, including:

- Hallucinations (false perceptions), which can occur in any sensory modality, although auditory hallucinations are most common, such as hearing voices;
- Delusions (erroneous beliefs), such as a conviction that one is being persecuted;
- Disorganized thinking ("formal thought disorder"), such as frequent derailment or incoherence; and
- Grossly disorganized or catatonic behavior, such as childlike silliness, unpredictable agitation, or a marked decrease in reactivity to the environment.

The positive symptoms may be further divided into the psychotic dimension (hallucinations and delusions) and the disorganized dimension (disorganized speech and behavior).

Negative symptoms may also be present, marked by a decrease in or loss of normal functions. The *DSM-IV-TR* negative symptoms include:

- Affective flattening, which is marked by restrictions in the range and intensity of emotional expression;
- Alogia, which is marked by restrictions in the fluency and productivity of thought and speech; and
- Avolition, which is marked by restrictions in the initiation of goal-directed behavior.

These positive and negative symptoms result in impairment in one or more major areas of functioning, such as school, work, relationships, or self-care.

In addition to positive and negative symptoms, some experts also emphasize the cognitive difficulties associated with schizophrenia (e.g., Mueser & Gingerich, 2006). Cognitive difficulties may affect attention and concentration, information-processing speed, memory and learning, executive functions, and social cognition. Such problems can have a significant impact on social, educational, and employment functioning.

It is generally believed that childhood schizophrenia is simply an early version of the adult disorder (Torrey, 2006). As the American Academy of Child & Adolescent Psychiatry (AACAP; http://www .aacap.org/) points out, however, the symptoms and behavior of young patients may differ from those of adults. Thus, clinicians need to share the general diagnostic criteria with families while monitoring the particular symptomatic pattern. The AACAP Web site specifies the symptoms and behaviors that can occur in children or adolescents with schizophrenia:

- Seeing things and hearing voices that are not real;
- Odd and eccentric behavior or speech;
- Unusual or bizarre thoughts;
- Confusing television and dreams with reality;

- Confused thinking;
- Extreme moodiness;
- A belief that people are out to get them or are talking about them;
- Severe anxiety and fearfulness;
- Difficulty relating to peers and keeping friends;
- Withdrawal and increased isolation; and
- A decline in personal hygiene.

The behavior of some young people with schizophrenia may change slowly over time. In other cases, the onset may appear to be sudden, although earlier signs can often be seen in retrospect. For some individuals, the symptoms remain chronic or get worse, whereas for others they may improve. Complete remission is not common, although many individuals recover sufficiently to enjoy fulfilling lives. Of those who remain ill, some have a relatively stable course, but others experience a more turbulent and debilitating path.

Schizophrenia—more appropriately referred to as the schizophrenias—is characterized by considerable heterogeneity in etiology, onset, symptoms, course, and prognosis (Torrey, 2006). Reflecting this variability, *DSM-IV-TR* specifies five types of schizophrenia:

- Paranoid type, which is marked by the presence of prominent delusions or auditory hallucinations in the context of a relative preservation of cognitive functioning and affect;
- Disorganized type, which is marked by disorganized speech, disorganized behavior, and flat or inappropriate affect;
- Catatonic type, which is marked by psychomotor disturbance that may involve motoric immobility; excessive motor activity; extreme negativism, such as maintenance of a rigid posture; peculiarities of voluntary movement, such as inappropriate or bizarre postures; and echolalia or echopraxia;
- Undifferentiated type, in which symptoms meet the diagnostic criteria for schizophrenia but not the criteria for paranoid, disorganized, or catatonic types; and

- Residual type, when there has been at least one episode of schizophrenia in the past, but the current clinical picture does not include prominent positive symptoms.

There are two other related disorders listed in *DSM-IV-TR*. The first is *schizoaffective disorder*, which is characterized by the presence a major depressive, manic, or mixed episode, as well as concurrent symptoms of schizophrenia. The second is *schizophreniform disorder*, in which the essential features are identical to those of schizophrenia, but the duration is less than 6 months.

In her memoir, *The Center Cannot Hold*, law professor Elyn Saks (2007) provided an eloquent—and harrowing—account of her life with schizophrenia. She described the onset of the illness when "schizophrenia rolls in like a slow fog, becoming imperceptibly thicker as time goes on" (p. 35). She wrote about her experience of paranoia, her inability to distinguish between imaginary fears and real ones, and her struggle with terrifying auditory hallucinations. "My psychosis is a waking nightmare, in which my demons are so terrifying that all my angels have already fled" (p. 336). But, her book is also a hopeful account of a journey that is marked by many accomplishments and that culminates in a full, rich, and satisfying life.

Risk Factors

There is strong evidence for the role of biological factors in schizophrenia, although the etiological picture is complex. Important biological factors include:

- Genetic factors, with strong evidence from family, adoption, and twin studies that close relatives of people with schizophrenia are at increased risk for developing the disorder;
- Neurochemical factors, such as neurotransmitter abnormalities; and

- Neurobiological factors, such as abnormal brain structure and function.

As Torrey (2006) reported, there is also evidence for the possible role of other biological factors, including neuropsychological deficits, neurological abnormalities, electrical abnormalities, and immunological and inflammatory abnormalities. In addition, he noted that individuals with schizophrenia have been born disproportionately in the winter and spring, that they are more prevalent in urban areas, and that other abnormalities are sometimes present, such as pregnancy and birth complications, minor physical anomalies, and an absence of rheumatoid arthritis.

In addition to biological risk factors, there is general agreement that stress can affect the course of schizophrenia, have an adverse impact on functioning, and increase the risk of a relapse (Mueser & Gingerich, 2006). Thus, the vulnerability–stress model offers a useful way of integrating current thinking about schizophrenia. The model assumes that the disorder involves a biogenetic vulnerability or predisposition to develop the disorder. A range of biological and psychosocial factors can interact with this vulnerability to affect the manifestation and course of the illness. Risk factors, such as stress, are associated with symptom exacerbation and increased likelihood of relapse. Protective factors, such as effective stress management strategies, can ameliorate the symptoms of the disorder and make relapse less likely.

Torrey (2006) estimated that approximately one quarter to one third of those who later develop schizophrenia are different as children. These differences include delayed developmental milestones in infancy, more language and speech problems, poorer coordination, poorer academic achievement, poorer social functioning, and fewer friends. He cautioned that these childhood precursors are merely statistical associations and are not predictors for individual cases. In fact, most children with these problems do not develop schizophrenia.

Torrey (2006) also discussed the prognostic signs that are associated with good and poor outcomes, again emphasizing that these are merely statistical associations that do not predict individual outcomes. The following are associated with a good outcome: relatively normal childhood, female, no family history of schizophrenia, older age at onset, sudden onset, paranoid or catatonic symptoms, presence of normal emotions, good awareness of illness, normal results of brain-imaging tests, and good initial response to medication.

Summarizing results of long-term studies, Torrey (2006) reported that 30 years after a diagnosis of schizophrenia, 25% of individuals are completely recovered, 35% are much improved and relatively independent, 15% are improved but require an extensive support network, 10% are hospitalized and unimproved, and 15% are dead, most often from suicide. Thus, over time, a majority of individuals with schizophrenia recover sufficiently to lead meaningful, rewarding, and productive lives (see Davidson, Harding, & Spaniol, 2005). As is well established, however, the journey is a challenging one for those with schizophrenia, particularly children and adolescents, and for their families.

Although fewer outcome studies have been conducted with young people, Volkmar and Tsatsanis (2002) stated that the outcome for childhood-onset schizophrenia tends to be poor. Many young patients experience persistent impairment, although about half of children show substantial improvement, and about one third remain in remission. They reported that better outcomes are associated with acute onset, older age at onset, good premorbid adjustment, and well-differentiated symptomatology. It is important to note, however, that these older long-term studies do not reflect current developments in treatment.

Treatment

Numerous evidence-based treatments are now available for schizophrenia, although most of the research has been conducted with adults. As Gur and Johnson (2006) pointed out, most of the progressive deterioration that can occur with schizophrenia takes place within the first 5 to 10 years after the initial psychotic episode. Thus, early identification and treatment are essential and can prevent the worst effects over the long term. Unfortunately, as the authors noted, many people with schizophrenia do not go willingly to treatment at the first signs of the illness, possibly because they feel their delusions and hallucinations are real and do not require treatment. Moreover, even when families have obtained a comprehensive evaluation, the initial treatment may not prove successful, and teenagers may be very reluctant to remain on medication. In response to these challenges, Gur and Johnson encouraged parents to be persistent in obtaining an evaluation, advocating for their child, and supporting the treatment plan.

A cornerstone of any treatment plan for schizophrenia is the use of antipsychotic medication. Among adults, benefits of antipsychotic medication include decreased symptoms, reduced risk of relapse, and increased response to psychosocial interventions (Mueser, Torrey, Lynde, Singer, & Drake, 2003). There are also some promising results with younger patients (Volkmar & Tsatsanis, 2002). As Gur and Johnson (2006) discussed, most studies have found antipsychotic medication results in improvement in positive symptoms for about 70% of patients; medication is less effective in reducing negative symptoms.

Gur and Johnson (2006) noted that when they became available in the 1990s, second-generation atypical antipsychotic medications became the drug of choice for the treatment of schizophrenia, especially for young people. Some atypical antipsychotics include Abilify, Clozaril, Geodon, Seroquel, Risperdal, and Zyprexa. These newer antipsychotics are associated with fewer serious side effects, such as effects related to the extrapyramidal system (EPS), appear to work as well as the older drugs, are sometimes effective against negative symptoms, and are better tolerated by patients. The authors also pointed out that the newer antipsychotics also have side effects, such as sedation and significant weight gain, and that finding the most effective medication may take time and experimentation. Given the importance of medication in the treatment of schizophrenia, families need to be well informed about the prescribed medication.

In her memoir of life with schizophrenia, Saks (2007) talked about her experience with one of these atypical antipsychotics. After many years of treatment with older medications, she began to take Zyprexa:

> The change was fast and dramatic. First, the side effects were much less. . . . Instead of being groggy or feeling tired, I felt alert and rested, energetic in a way I hadn't felt in a long time—so long, in fact, that I'd almost forgotten what those good feelings were like. . . . The clinical result was, not to overstate it, like daylight dawning after a long night—I could see the world in a way I'd never seen it before. (p. 303)

Because medications are constantly being developed, it is important for clinicians and families to keep abreast of new developments, which may offer more effective medications with fewer side effects, target negative symptoms and cognitive deficits, and gain greater patient acceptance. In the meantime, adolescents with schizophrenia may be disinclined to follow the medication regime, a reluctance that poses problems for them, for their families, and for clinicians. Gur and Johnson (2006) estimated that nonadherence rates for oral antipsychotic medication are somewhere between 15% and 35% among hospitalized patients and as high as 65% among outpatients; such rates are somewhat lower among patients on long-acting injectables.

Generally combined with medication, as Mueser and his colleagues (2003) discussed, effective psychosocial interventions are also available for the treatment of schizophrenia. They reported that in studies with adults, psychosocial interventions have demonstrated benefits in the areas of relapse and rehospitalization, housing stability, competitive employment, social functioning, psychotic symptoms, and substance use disorders. The authors provided an overview of some evidence-based psychosocial interventions, including assertive community treatment (ACT), family psychoeducation, supported employment, illness management and recovery skills, and integrated dual disorders treatment.

The ACT model was developed to meet the needs of individuals with a history of high service utilization or severe functional impairment. Services are provided on a 24-hour basis in natural living environments by multidisciplinary treatment and rehabilitation teams. Family psychoeducation generally includes services both for people with schizophrenia and for their family members. Components include education about mental illness and its management, skills training, and social support. Supported employment features rapid job search rather than extensive prevocational assessment, competitive wages for jobs in integrated settings, ongoing support once a job has been obtained, and combined vocational and mental health services.

Interventions that target illness management and recovery are designed to help people with schizophrenia acquire the information and skills needed to collaborate in their treatment, to minimize the effects of the disorder on their lives, and to be able to pursue personally meaningful goals. Integrated dual disorders treatment focuses on substance use disorder, which is the most common and clinically significant comorbidity associated with schizophrenia. Integrated mental health and substance abuse programs provide simultaneous treatment of both disorders in a single setting.

Although these psychosocial interventions are evidence-based treatments for adults who have schizophrenia, with strong empirical support for their effectiveness, there has been relatively little research concerned with children and adolescents. Nevertheless, some of these interventions may be helpful for young patients. For example, family psychoeducation is essential for these struggling families, as is an age-appropriate form of illness management training that helps adolescents acquire the information and skills needed to collaborate in their treatment, minimize the effects of the disorder on their lives, and pursue their goals.

Gur and Johnson (2006) described some psychosocial interventions that have been adapted for adolescents with schizophrenia and noted that there are some promising research findings. These interventions include:

- Supportive psychotherapy, which is intended to provide a corrective emotional experience, thereby enhancing stability and healthy problem solving;
- Behavior therapy, which is designed to decrease maladaptive behavior and increase desirable behavior, such as social skills and self-care;
- Cognitive remediation therapy, which focuses on cognitive difficulties in attention, learning, and memory;
- Group therapy, which is a natural setting for adolescents, although this intervention may be damaging for fragile adolescents; and
- Family therapy, which may be useful for families with multiple problems.

Particularly with disorders like schizophrenia that are severe and persistent, adolescents and families need comprehensive and individualized services that can address their ongoing needs and empower them in dealing with this devastating illness over the long term.

Helping Families Cope With Schizophrenia

Some excellent resources are available for families, although most focus on adults with schizophrenia. Nevertheless, these resources contain a wealth of information about schizophrenia and family coping strategies. As noted, because this area of research and practice is changing rapidly, older resources should be avoided. For example, some earlier publications incorporated unsupported assumptions about family pathogenesis and dysfunction, which are inconsistent with the evidence for the importance of biological factors and are also harmful to families, who may feel blamed for the illness. Moreover, earlier resources may incorrectly characterize schizophrenia as an inevitably debilitating and deteriorating disorder, which is counter to results of long-term studies and is likely to engender feelings of hopelessness and helplessness in patients and families—as well as clinicians.

An excellent book for families that does focus on adolescents is *If Your Adolescent Has Schizophrenia: An Essential Resource for Parents* (Gur & Johnson, 2006). The authors offered a "whole-family approach" to adolescent schizophrenia that highlights the importance of recognizing symptoms, getting a diagnosis, obtaining treatment, managing the illness, and maintaining wellness. Useful adult-oriented books include *The Complete Family Guide to Schizophrenia* (Mueser & Gingerich, 2006); *The Family Intervention Guide to Mental Illness* (Morey & Mueser, 2007); and *Surviving Schizophrenia* (Torrey, 2006). Topics covered in these books include understanding the illness, causes of schizophrenia, the course of the disorder, treatments for schizophrenia, survival strategies for patients and families, reducing symptoms and relapses, learning about recovery, improving family relationships, improving family problem solving, and planning for the future. Several family-focused professional books are also available, including *Serious Mental Illness and the Family: The Practitioner's Guide* (Marsh, 1998) and *A Family-Focused Approach to Serious Mental Illness: Empirically Supported Interventions* (Marsh, 2001). As we discuss in Chapter 11, the principles of effective family-focused intervention in mental illness apply to patients of all ages.

In addition, family advocacy groups such as the National Alliance on Mental Illness (NAMI; http://www.nami.org/) and Mental Health America (http://www.nmha.org/) are a valuable resource for families. As a large national organization with affiliates throughout the United States, NAMI offers a range of services for families, including support groups, a free 12-week educational program, conferences, and an informative Web site.

Helping Adolescents Cope With Schizophrenia at Home

Although maintaining a supportive environment is important for all families who include a child with mental illness, the home environment is especially important for those with schizophrenia. In discussing the vulnerability–stress model of schizophrenia, Mueser and Gingerich (2006) suggested that the severity and course of symptoms are determined by four factors: biological vulnerability, stress, coping skills, and social support. As people with schizophrenia learn to cope more effectively with stress, they become less vulnerable to symptoms and better able to enjoy life. Thus, effective interventions assist all members of the family to identify sources of stress, to recognize signs of stress, and to manage stress by reducing the sources of stress and developing stress management skills. In fact, researchers have found that assisting families to achieve and maintain a low-stress environment reduces the risk of relapse and rehospitalization.

Likewise, as discussed, good communication, problem-solving, and assertiveness skills are important for all families dealing with child and adolescent mental illness. Many of the coping strategies already discussed are applicable to schizophrenia, including the generic strategies discussed in Chapter 6, such as creating a supportive family environment, taking care of themselves, empowering their family, distinguishing between the child and the disorder, adapting their parenting style, establishing realistic expectations, maintaining a balance that meets the needs of all family members, meeting the needs of well siblings, preparing for crises, and maintaining a hopeful attitude.

By sharing information from publications and other resources concerned with schizophrenia, practitioners can help families:

- Set clear, simple rules;
- Develop realistic expectations for the adolescent, who may spend considerable time and energy coping with the symptoms of schizophrenia;

- Realize that people with schizophrenia may not recognize ("lack of insight") that they have a mental illness, especially at the onset;
- Recognize that schizophrenia is not a character flaw but a neurobiological disorder;
- Recognize that schizophrenia is a persistent condition that is typically marked by acute episodes from time to time;
- Offer the teenager an opportunity to talk about the symptoms of schizophrenia;
- Provide assistance in developing skills for coping with anxiety, which is commonly associated with schizophrenia;
- Avoid becoming discouraged if it takes weeks or even months for the adolescent to be stabilized on medication;
- Be patient and persistent in finding quality care, which make take some time and energy;
- Recognize that stress may exacerbate symptoms and require a change in medication dosage; and
- Be prepared for relapse and have a crisis plan ready to activate in an emergency.

Clinicians can also help families cope effectively with the positive, negative, and cognitive symptoms of schizophrenia. In response to positive symptoms, parents should:

- Avoid taking the delusions personally (e.g., when the child claims that the parent is the devil)—it is the illness talking;
- Respond in a way that respects the teenager's dignity and acknowledges the terror that often accompanies psychosis without reinforcing the symptoms;
- Recognize that people with schizophrenia often experience hallucinations and delusions as real, although with time they may learn to recognize these experiences as symptoms of their disorder;
- Understand that it is not helpful to argue with teenagers about the reality of their hallucinations and delusions—parents are not likely to convince them they are wrong, and the conflict will be stressful for both parties; and

- Remain nonjudgmental while responding to the adolescent's concerns (e.g., "I'm sure that must upset you" or "Can I do anything to make you feel better?").

Families also need to recognize the negative symptoms of schizophrenia as part of the illness, such as lack of motivation, inability to follow through on tasks, inability to experience pleasure and to enjoy relationships, inability to feel and express emotions, inability to focus on activities, and impoverished thought and speech.

Likewise, families need to be familiar with the cognitive symptoms of schizophrenia (see Mueser & Gingerich, 2006).

- For problems in attention and concentration, encourage the adolescent to schedule regular breaks, remove distractions, and gradually improve attention span by increasing the duration of work periods.
- For slow information-processing speed, help the teenager avoid rushing and allow time to complete tasks.
- For problems in learning and memory, suggest compensatory strategies, such as the use of memory aids (e.g., a written list), memory-sharpening strategies (e.g., repeating important information), a daily schedule, and overlearning, which involves extensive practice.
- For problems in executive functions, match daily tasks to the adolescent's cognitive skills, schedule problem-solving meetings, and use literal rather than abstract language.
- For problems in social cognition, provide assistance in recognizing facial expressions, using explicit feeling statements, and understanding social norms.

Helping Adolescents Cope With Schizophrenia in School

Given the severity of schizophrenia, families are likely to spend considerable time working with school personnel to develop an appropriate educational plan. It is important for school personnel to be well informed about schizophrenia so that they can discuss concerns with students and families. As noted, students with mental illness should be encouraged and reinforced for functioning as normally as possible in a regular classroom. As Gur and Johnson (2006) pointed out, however, schizophrenia is associated with many potential problems that may affect academic performance, including the following: inability to screen out environmental stimuli, inability to concentrate, difficulty interacting with others, difficulty handling negative feedback, and difficulty adjusting to change.

In addition to the school-based interventions mentioned in Chapter 6, some school-based strategies are specifically designed to manage the symptoms of schizophrenia and to target problems in time management, memory, concentration, organization and prioritization, social skills, completing course requirements, and test taking. See the work of Gur and Johnson (2006) and the information provided by the Massachusetts General Hospital School Psychiatry Program & MADI Resource Center on their Web site (http://www.massgeneral .org/schoolpsychiatry/). In addition, if appropriate, school personnel can:

- Identify and avoid exposure to known distressing stimuli;
- Provide the student with grounding activities, such as familiar, predictable activities;
- Allow the student alternative schoolwork or activities to avoid provoking delusions;
- Devise steps to employ when the student experiences delusions or hallucinations, such as a series of steps to deescalate (e.g., change the topic, activity, setting, or staff);
- Provide a hierarchy of safe places to go if the student is overstimulated; or
- Offer prearranged breaks to help the student manage anxiety, stress, or extreme restlessness caused by medication.

Anthony Poulos: The Treatment Plan

Returning to Anthony Poulos and his family, Anthony has already received a diagnosis of paranoid schizophrenia. As specified in the treatment plan, the long-term goals are to assist Anthony and his family to understand and accept his schizophrenia, to engage them in the treatment plan, to help them manage the symptoms of the disorder, and to support Anthony in achieving his personal objectives. The individualized treatment plan might include the following interventions:

- Refer Anthony for a medication consult to determine is he is an appropriate candidate for antipsychotic medication.
- Provide family psychoeducation for the Poulos family to educate them about schizophrenia and its treatment, to strengthen their coping skills, and to offer support.
- Provide an age-appropriate form of illness management training to help Anthony acquire the information and skills needed to collaborate in his treatment, to minimize the effects of the disorder on his life, and to assist him in achieving his goals.
- Provide cognitive remediation therapy for problems in attention, learning, and memory.
- Provide individual psychotherapy to help Anthony come to terms with his illness and enhance his stability.
- Help Anthony and his family identify early warning signs and triggers of his symptoms.
- Work with Anthony and his family to implement these strategies at home and to develop relapse prevention and crisis plans.
- Collaborate with the school in developing an Individualized Education Plan (IEP) that provides regular breaks to help Anthony manage medication-related restlessness, specifies steps to employ when he is experiencing psychotic symptoms, allows modified assignments and examinations to accommodate his cognitive limitations, offers weekly sessions with a school counselor to help him manage school-

related stress, provides home-based assistance following relapse or hospitalization, and initiates transitional planning.

In addition, the practitioner can work with the Poulos family in developing a family service plan that can help them to identify and prioritize their needs, to deal with illness-related concerns, to undertake long-term planning, and to make an informed choice about their use of other available services. For example, the family might choose a referral to a local affiliate of NAMI that offers educational programs and support groups; individual sessions for Sophia, who has experienced significant distress as a result of Anthony's illness; as-needed sessions for his parents to deal with ongoing concerns; and consultation with school personnel regarding transitional planning.

Working With the Poulos Family

Psychologist Peter Rafferty is a member of a group practice that includes a psychiatrist and a social worker. The group has hospital privileges at a local hospital that has an adolescent inpatient unit. The psychiatrist conducted an evaluation of Anthony during his hospitalization and provided the diagnosis to his parents, Lynne and Nicholas Poulos.

Dr. Rafferty: Hello, Mr. and Mrs. Poulos. I appreciate your taking time off from work to meet with me about Anthony. As you know, I'll be following up with his outpatient therapy. I'm sorry I didn't have an opportunity to meet with you when Anthony was discharged. I was out of town at a conference. But, I'm sure you have many questions, and I also want to share our recommendations for treatment.

Nicholas: All they told us at the hospital was Anthony's diagnosis of paranoid schizophrenia. No one explained what that meant or what the future holds.

Dr. Rafferty: I'm really sorry that you received so little information. In my absence, another staff member should have met with you. I realize it's difficult enough to hear that your son has schizophrenia. I'll work with you in helping you obtain the information and skills you need to help Anthony and to help the rest of your family. Schizophrenia is a devastating illness that affects all members of the family, but there is much reason for hope. We now have many effective treatments for schizophrenia that can help individuals like Anthony learn to manage their illness and go on with their lives.

Lynne: Are you going to explain the treatments and show us how we can help our son?

Dr. Rafferty: Yes, that's one of the things I want to do today. But, first I want to provide some information about schizophrenia and its symptoms, which fall into three general areas. Positive symptoms include hallucinations or false perceptions, such as hearing voices, and delusions or erroneous beliefs, such as a belief that other people are planning to harm you. Another positive symptom is very disorganized thinking or behavior, such as speech that seems to make no sense, what we sometimes call *word salad*—just a jumble of words that don't have any real meaning.

Lynne: We've certainly seen those positive symptoms with Anthony, who has said he hears voices and claims people are plotting against him.

Nicholas: He says and does things that seem crazy. When I tell him that the voices aren't real and that no one is plotting against him, he just gets more upset and insists I am wrong.

Dr. Rafferty: As you have seen, especially at the onset of the illness, people with schizophrenia often think their hallucinations and delusions are real. Eventually, they may learn that their false perceptions and beliefs are symptoms of schizophrenia, but that usually takes time and patience.

Lynne: What are the other symptoms?

Dr. Rafferty: Negative symptoms involve a decrease in or loss of normal functions. These symptoms may include lack of motivation, inability to follow through on tasks, inability to experience pleasure and to enjoy relationships, inability to feel and express emotions, inability to focus on activities, and impoverished thought and speech. The third category is cognitive symptoms, which affect attention and concentration, information-processing speed, memory and learning, executive functions such as the ability to develop an effective plan, and social cognition such as the ability to interpret facial expressions. The positive, negative, and cognitive symptoms of schizophrenia typically have a significant impact on all areas of life, including school, relationships, and self-care, as they have in Anthony's case.

Lynne: We've seen many of these symptoms, although we didn't know they were symptoms of a mental illness. And, they have had a harmful effect on Anthony's schoolwork and our home life. But, how can Anthony be helped?

Dr. Rafferty: We have many effective treatments for schizophrenia, including antipsychotic medication that can reduce his symptoms. As you know, Anthony has begun to take a relatively new medication that is generally effective in controlling the symptoms of schizophrenia, especially hallucinations and delusions. I know you received some information about the medication when he was an inpatient, but I want to review information about the medication and help you monitor his response to medication and possible side effects. I'll also be working closely with Anthony to monitor his medication. Sometimes, we need to change or combine medications, so we all need to be patient until we find what works best for him.

Nicholas: We'll go over this information and make a list of questions for our next visit.

Dr. Rafferty: Although medication can reduce Anthony's symptoms, we also want to help him move on with his life. We have already started to offer him illness management training that can help him acquire the information and skills needed to collaborate in his treatment, to minimize the effects of the disorder on his life, and to assist him in achieving his goals. In addition, we plan to provide cognitive remediation therapy for his problems in attention, learning, and memory and to provide individual psychotherapy to help him come to terms with his illness and improve his stability.

Nicholas: Do these treatments really work with teens as sick as Anthony?

Dr. Rafferty: Yes, we have strong evidence that these treatments do help patients like Anthony. But, individuals respond differently, so we'll have to see how much improvement he experiences. Here are some research reports that discuss various treatments for schizophrenia and the evidence for their effectiveness.

Lynne: What about the rest of our family? We need to know how to help Anthony. And it's been very difficult for his sister, Sophia, to see Anthony get so sick. She's confused and sometimes frightened by his behavior.

Dr. Rafferty: I believe the best way to help Anthony is to work with your entire family. I would like to schedule a session with Sophia so I can provide information about schizophrenia and answer her questions. Siblings often suffer along with their brother or sister, and I want to make sure we meet her needs. I also want to hold some family sessions with all of you, including Anthony, to help you identify the early warning signs and triggers of his symptoms. That will allow us to intervene early if his symptoms seem to be returning or getting worse. Early intervention can reduce the risk of relapse and perhaps avoid a crisis or hospitalization.

Lynne: Anthony's grandmother, Eleni, lives with us. But, she speaks very little English, even after all these years in the country. So, it would be best if she did not attend the family session. My husband is bilingual, so he can explain it to my mother-in-law, and I can also communicate fairly well with her.

Dr. Rafferty: That makes sense. In addition to our services, Anthony may be eligible for special education services. Here is some material on the special education process. If you would like me to, I can write a report that our social worker can provide to the multidisciplinary team at school. I'll also work with you in developing some possible school-based interventions that you can discuss with the school. Since he is a senior, we can work with the school in developing a transition plan designed to determine which services Anthony will need after his graduation. We'll work with you and Anthony to help him establish a set of realistic goals and to access the services, resources, and supports that are needed to achieve his goals.

Lynne: We would appreciate a report that can be shared with the school as well as any recommendations you feel would be helpful.

Dr. Rafferty: We've covered an awful lot today. You must feel a bit overwhelmed.

Nicholas: There seems to be so much to learn. But, this has been very helpful, and we'll read the materials you have provided. I wish someone had provided this information when Anthony was in the hospital. That was such a difficult time for all of us. But for the first time in months, I'm beginning to believe there is hope for Anthony and for our family.

Dr. Rafferty: Again, I'm sorry no one at the hospital talked with you about Anthony's diagnosis and treatment plan. I know how important that is for families and will follow up to see why that didn't take place. But, as I mentioned, with so many effective treatments for schizophrenia, there is ample reason to hope for improvement. We'll need your help as we move forward. A caring and knowledgeable family is Anthony's best resource. The last thing I want to mention is a list I've developed of books, Web sites, and community resources that you might find helpful. We can talk more about these when you come in for your appointment next week.

FAMILY–PROFESSIONAL COLLABORATION

CHAPTER ELEVEN

Effective Family-Focused Services

The family of Nina Montague includes three generations. Her grandparents, Alberto and Carmela, emigrated from Cuba with their three sons. They originally lived with relatives in Miami, but eventually established a successful Cuban restaurant and raised their sons in their own home. Their sons all graduated from college and established careers in the Miami area. The oldest, Raul, married his college sweetheart, Isabel, and began working as an engineer to support his family. For a decade, Isabel stayed home to care for their three children, 15-year-old Maria, 13-year-old Ernesto, and 11-year-old Nina. When Isabel returned to work as a nurse, the now-retired grandparents joined the household to help out with the children. The extended family prospered, enjoying their lives and their family. Then, as Isabel said later, everything changed when Nina was in a harrowing automobile accident. She and three friends were being driven to a gymnastics class by one girl's mother when they were struck head-on by an out-of-control pickup truck. One of Nina's friends was transported by helicopter to a hospital with a trauma unit, where she later died. The remaining passengers, including Nina, were rushed by ambulance to the local hospital, where they were treated for serious injuries. Although all four eventually recovered, Nina was transformed by the terrifying experience. Once a happy and affectionate child, she was now fearful and easily startled, became extremely upset when she had to travel by car, complained of intrusive memories and flashbacks, and had great difficulty sleeping. Recognizing the symptoms of posttraumatic stress disorder, Nina's pediatrician referred the family to the local mental health center. The entire family was affected by Nina's problems, absorbing her pain and wondering what the future held.

As is apparent in the case of Nina Montague, there is a compelling rationale for a family-focused approach to the treatment of child and adolescent mental illness. First, families serve not only as primary caregivers but also as informal case managers, de facto crisis intervention specialists, and advocates for their child. Second, families can play a constructive role in supporting the treatment plan and in developing and implementing home- and school-based interventions. Third, given the severity and persistence of early-onset mental illness, these families have compelling needs of their own for information, skills, and support. Finally, several interventions offer potential benefits for families, including family psychoeducation, family education, family consultation, family support and advocacy groups, and family therapy.

We begin this chapter with a discussion of professional competencies, followed by a consideration of family engagement and assessment, family intervention models, some professional issues, and the family service plan. Finally, we return to the Montague family and suggest a possible service plan.

Professional Competencies

Reflecting the increased emphasis on professional competence (Rubin et al., 2007), in this section we discuss the competencies needed for effective practice in the area of early-onset mental illness. Professional practice in this area requires all of the basic competencies used by child and adolescent practitioners on a daily basis (see Hansen et al., 1999; Roberts et al., 1998). Our focus is not on these general competencies but on the specialized knowledge, skills, and attitudes needed for working with children and adolescents who have serious mental illness and with their families.

Knowledge

Knowledge involves mastery of information required for professional practice. When working in this area, practitioners need knowledge of:

- Diagnostic criteria and characteristics of severe mental disorders among children and adolescents;
- Current thinking regarding the etiology and life-span developmental course of these disorders;
- Child, adolescent, and family assessment methods for these disorders;
- Child, adolescent, parent, family, and community psychosocial interventions for these disorders, as well as their empirical foundations;
- Psychopharmacological interventions for these disorders, as well as their empirical foundations;
- The experiences and needs of these children, adolescents, and families;
- Child-serving systems and their role in intervention;
- Community resources, such as family advocacy organizations;
- Professional, ethical, and legal issues of special concern regarding childhood mental illness; and
- Social, cultural, ethnic, gender, and other issues of special concern with mental illness.

Skills

Knowledge alone does not guarantee competence; understanding first must be translated into practice. Skills involve the ability to use knowledge effectively and readily in performance. In the area of early-onset mental illness, practitioners need to be able to:

- Engage families in a manner that respects their dignity;
- Establish partnerships with families;
- Communicate effectively with all members of the family;
- Assist families to prioritize and meet their own needs;
- Develop an individualized treatment plan for the child or adolescent;
- Provide evidence-based child and adolescent psychosocial interventions;
- Collaborate with psychopharmacologists regarding medication;
- Develop an individualized service plan for the family unit;
- Provide the full range of family interventions;
- Provide culturally competent assessment, diagnosis, treatment planning, and intervention;
- Adapt their style to a particular family;
- Collaborate with members of multidisciplinary treatment teams; and
- Access community resources and provide community interventions.

Attitudes

Attitudes are cognitive or emotional reactions to individuals, objects, or situations. As we have discussed, practitioners need to adopt a strength-based approach to professional practice that emphasizes individual, family, and community strengths. In addition, clinicians can enhance their effectiveness by adopting a model of family-driven care. As defined by the National Federation of Families for Children's Mental Health (2008; http://ffcmh.org/), *family-driven* means that families have a primary decision-making role in the care of their own children and in the policies and procedures that govern the mental health care of all children. This includes:

- Choosing supports, services, and providers;
- Setting goals;

- Designing and implementing programs;
- Monitoring outcomes;
- Partnering in funding decisions; and
- Determining the effectiveness of efforts to promote the mental health and well-being of children and youth.

Families and young people who feel they are an integral part in a family-driven system of care are more likely to be fully engaged in treatment. Other facilitative attitudes include the following:

- Tolerance and respect for these children, adolescents, and families;
- A sense of hopefulness that can counteract the feelings of despair and helplessness so often associated with child and adolescent mental illness;
- Compassion and empathy for individuals and families affected by these disorders;
- Emphasis on children and adolescents as whole persons who are not defined by their illness;
- Emphasis on family well-being and satisfaction with services;
- Absence of labeling and blame;
- Appreciation of the ethnocultural context of early-onset mental illness;
- Sensitivity to the stigmatization and discrimination associated with mental illness in our society; and
- Willingness to work with families as advocates for a more responsive system of care.

Engaging and Assessing Families

Particularly at the time of the initial diagnosis and during crises, these families often feel distressed, confused, and overwhelmed. Clinicians can establish rapport by listening to their stories and by assisting families to identify and prioritize their needs, deal with illness-related concerns, and make an informed choice about their use of available services. Families often appreciate handouts about mental illness and suggestions for family resources, such as those mentioned in previous chapters (e.g., Foa & Andrews, 2006; Fristad & Arnold, 2004; Gur & Johnson, 2006; Miklowitz & George, 2008; Morey & Mueser, 2007).

An initial family assessment enables practitioners to respond to any urgent needs and begin formulating a family service plan (see Mueser & Glynn, 1999). Assessment usually covers the following:

- Current issues facing the family, such as the risk of harm to their child or to others;
- Their knowledge of mental illness, including any misconceptions they have;
- Their skills for coping with the illness and with family stress in general;
- Their strengths, resources, and potential contributions to their child's treatment;
- The impact of mental illness on their family unit and on individual members, including siblings;
- Other past or present problems that may affect the family's ability to cope with the illness;
- The level of support available to the family; and
- Their immediate and long-term needs and goals.

Family Intervention Models

Many of the adult-oriented family interventions available for serious mental illness can be adapted for clinical practice with children and adolescents (see Marsh, 1998, 2001; Marsh & Lefley, 2009). These include family psychoeducation, family education, family consultation, family support and advocacy groups, and family therapy.

Family Psychoeducation

Based on numerous well-designed studies, family psychoeducation is considered one of the major evidence-based practices for serious mental illness (Dixon, McFarlane, et al., 2001), including schizophrenia (Kuipers, Birchwood, & McCreadie, 2002) and bipolar disorder (Miklowitz et al., 2002). The core content of family psychoeducation is support for families, state-of-the-art education about serious mental illness, illness management strategies, problem-solving techniques, and resource information. Although family psychoeducation has generally been offered to families of adult patients, Fristad and Arnold (2004) have developed a psychoeducational model for child and adolescent mood disorders.

Family Education

Family education offers a shorter-term intervention designed to increase the knowledge of families and enhance their well-being. For example, the National Alliance on Mental Illness (NAMI; http://www.nami.org) has developed a 12-week Family-to-Family Education Program that has been offered nationally to thousands of families. The program, which is manualized and constantly updated, is presented by trained family members who teach other families about the causes and treatment of major mental illnesses and help them enhance their problem-solving skills. Evaluation of the program's effectiveness is currently under way, although preliminary results point to significant benefits for families (Dixon, Stewart, et al., 2001).

Family Consultation

Family consultation assists families to identify and prioritize their needs, make an informed choice about services, and formulate a family service plan. As practiced by mental health professionals, family consultation has much in common with the consultative services offered by other professionals, such as accountants and attorneys. In each case, consultants offer expert knowledge, skills, and advice to families, who maintain primary responsibility for determining their own goals, for deciding whether to accept professional recommendations, and for implementing decisions. Family consultation may be limited to a specific request of families, such as concern about concurrent substance abuse or the risk of suicide. Ongoing consultation services may also be available as needed to deal with crises, life transitions, or other special needs. Although this adult-oriented intervention is rarely used in clinical practice today, partly because of problems with insurance reimbursement, this approach is appropriate for some younger families (Marsh & Lefley, 2003).

Family Support and Advocacy Groups

Time-limited family interventions cannot address unexpected problems that arise with cyclical mental disorders. Ongoing support groups, such as those offered by NAMI, provide considerable benefits for families. Reflecting research findings from adult-oriented multifamily groups, McFarlane, Hornby, Dixon, and McNary (2002) noted the benefits of shared experiences: Family groups normalize the experiences of families and offer resource information, exchange of coping strategies, a social network for isolated families, enhanced problem-solving capability, connections to advocacy organizations, and positive success stories with renewed hope for recovery. In a *New York Times* article, one mother affirmed the healing power of her support group: "In banding together to tell the truth about our own and our children's suffering, we have found resilience; and we have kept the terrible vacant loneliness at bay" (Schumacher, 2008, p. 6). Advocacy organizations such as NAMI welcome the involvement of family members who wish to move beyond mutual support and work to improve the mental health system by focusing on favorable legislation, funding for research and services, and stigma reduction.

Family Therapy

Family therapy may also be beneficial for some families. Families have essential needs for information, skills, and support. Once these needs have been met, some families may continue to experience significant problems. Any preexisting individual, marital, or family problems are likely to be exacerbated by illness-related stress. A parent might experience an unresolved grieving process, incapacitating feelings of guilt and responsibility, or inappropriate anger directed at the child. Spouses or partners might face significant illness-related conflict or other relational problems. A multiproblem family might be unable to support the child's treatment.

On the other hand, some families may manifest none of these problems but nevertheless prefer to meet their needs within the context of a confidential therapeutic relationship. Thus, some families may benefit from psychotherapy in addition to educational, skills-oriented, and supportive services. At the same time, practitioners should be sensitive to the risks of negative effects when they dispense general prescriptions of family therapy based on assumptions of family pathogenesis or dysfunction or that ignore the needs and desires of particular families (Marsh, 2001; Marsh & Lefley, 2009).

Professional Issues

When working with families of children and adolescents who have mental illness, clinicians need to be familiar with relevant professional and legal issues, including those that pertain to professional practice with young patients and to confidentiality.

Working With Children and Adolescents

Parents and guardians are generally authorized to make treatment decisions for children under age 14. In contrast, even if they reside at home, unless they meet the standards for involuntary emergency examination and treatment, adolescents age 18 and older have full legal status, including the right to initiate treatment, to withdraw from treatment, and to a confidential therapeutic relationship.

Problems are most likely to arise in clinical practice with adolescents between ages 14 and 18. State regulations vary for this age group and may vary within a state across inpatient, outpatient, and involuntary treatment as well as between private and public sectors. Consequently, it is important for both professionals and families to determine how state regulations apply in the case of a particular teenager. In some states, adolescents may have rights that conflict with the interests of their parents, such as the right to withdraw from treatment even when it is recommended by professionals and supported by their parents.

Confidentiality

In Chapter 4, we discussed the Family Educational Rights and Privacy Act (FERPA), which covers confidentiality in school settings. In clinical settings, confidentiality is the professional ethical standard that offers protection against unauthorized disclosures. This standard requires clinicians to discuss relevant limitations on confidentiality at the beginning of therapy and thereafter as new circumstances warrant. Limitations may result from the risk of imminent harm; from the presence of other people in marital, family, and group therapy; or from applicable laws, institutional rules, or professional or scientific relationships. Therapists also need to discuss any foreseeable uses of information generated through their services.

Professionals may disclose confidential information with the appropriate consent, unless prohibited by law. In the case of a child or adolescent, the consent process will vary depending on the age of the patient and the legal requirements of the state. For example, a state might mandate that adolescents age 14 or older shall control the release of their records if they understand the nature of documents to be released and the purpose of their release. For children who are younger than 14 years of age or who have been adjudicated legally incompetent, a parent or guardian typically exercises control over the release of records.

Without the consent of the patient, confidential information should be disclosed only as mandated by law. Whenever a conflict exists between confidentiality and the mandatory reporting requirements that govern suspected or discovered child abuse, for example, the reporting requirements take precedence. As a consequence, mandated reporters are required to breach confidentiality if they have reasonable cause to suspect on the basis of their professional training and experience that a child coming before them in their professional or official capacity is an abused child. Confidential information may also be disclosed where permitted by law for a valid purpose, such as to protect the patient or others from harm, to provide needed professional services, to obtain appropriate professional consultations, or to obtain payment for services. Again, depending on state regulations, these exceptions must be shared with patients age 14 or older and with their parents or guardians.

Practitioners are required to take reasonable precautions to maintain confidentiality. Written and oral reports should include only germane information, and information should be shared only for appropriate purposes and with relevant individuals. In addition, clinicians should maintain appropriate confidentiality in record keeping. Family members need to be informed at the outset about record-keeping practices as well as procedures necessary to release records and to disclose confidential information. When consulting with colleagues, professionals should protect the confidentiality of the relationship unless they have obtained the prior consent of the patient or the disclosure cannot be avoided, and they should share information only to the extent necessary to achieve the purposes of the consultation. In the case of multiple patients, each legally competent party needs to provide consent for disclosure of confidential information, as in the case of participants in family therapy.

It is important for clinicians to understand potential conflicts regarding confidentiality as well as the ways in which these conflicts can be resolved. Consider the case of an adolescent who refuses to remain in therapy if his or her parents are involved. In some settings, separate staff members can be assigned to work with the parents and to consult with the adolescent's therapist to enhance treatment planning and coordination. In all settings, parents should have an avenue to express their concerns and to share observations about the risk of imminent harm, indications of substance abuse, evidence of treatment or medication nonadherence, or other serious matters.

In most cases, potential conflicts can be resolved (see Marsh & Lefley, 2009). Professionals can employ a release of information form that specifies the information that will be shared. If the release form is presented at the right time (during a relatively calm period) and in the right manner (as something that will enhance treatment), most adolescents are willing to authorize the release of relevant information to their parents. In these circumstances, clinicians can function as mediators who negotiate the boundaries of confidentiality to meet the needs of particular adolescents and parents. Parents can generally understand the need of an adolescent for a confidential therapeutic relationship. Likewise, adolescents can usually understand the need of parents for information about treatment decisions that affect their child and family.

The Family Service Plan

Although families of children and adolescents may play a central role in their child's treatment plan, a separate service plan is designed to address the needs of families themselves (see Marsh, 1998, 2001). Depending on the results of assessment, the family's needs and desires, and the available services, the plan might include some combination of consultative, supportive, educational, skills-oriented, and psychotherapeutic services. Clinicians should request regular feedback from families to ensure that services are responsive to their changing needs.

Given the diversity among families as well as their shifting needs over time, there is no single service plan for all families or even for all members within a given family.

The overarching goal is to provide an optimal service match for particular families (see Dixon, Adams, & Lucksted, 2000). As families are empowered to cope effectively with mental illness, substantial benefits will accrue for the child and family, for professionals, and for society.

Maximizing Family Resilience

We wrote in this book about family resilience, which involves more than effective coping. Resilient families not only cope effectively but also do so with vitality and satisfaction. In their research on the characteristics of resilient families, McCubbin and McCubbin (1988) highlighted the importance of family coherence and family hardiness. Family *coherence* is a fundamental coping strategy employed in the management of family problems that is marked by acceptance, loyalty, pride, faith, trust, respect, caring, and shared values. Family *hardiness*, the family's internal strengths and durability, is distinguished by an internal sense of control of life events and hardships, a sense of meaningfulness in life, involvement in activities, and a commitment to learn and explore new and challenging experiences. Families who are high on family coherence and family hardiness are better able to manage the impact of family stressors and to recover from family crises.

Similarly, Walsh (2006) identified several keys to family resilience: (a) family belief systems, such as the ability to find meaning in adversity, a positive outlook, and transcendence and spirituality; (b) organization patterns, such as flexibility, connectedness, and social and economic resources; and (c) communication processes, such as clarity, open emotional expression, and collaborative problem solving. Specifically, resilient families find shared meaning in their adversity, mobilize their resources to counter stress and resolve problems, and communicate in a clear, direct, and supportive manner.

Employing a strength-based and collaborative approach with families, practitioners can assist them to assume ownership of their lives, face life's challenges with confidence, view the world in positive but realistic terms, treat each other with tolerance and respect, cherish their family bonds and commitments, reach out to others to give and receive support, emphasize their gains, and celebrate the good times. Working with these families, professionals can encourage resilient thinking and behavior among families and reinforce resilience when it does occur (Beavers & Hampson, 1990; Waters & Lawrence, 1993). Empowering families to meet their own needs, professionals can assist them to move from helplessness to hopefulness and to recapture their sense of joy and satisfaction.

As Walsh (2006) pointed out, it is important to note that family resilience occurs not *in spite of* crisis and challenge but *because of* adversity. Responding to disruptive events, resilient families reconstruct themselves in adaptive ways by acquiring new insights, knowledge, and skills; developing greater confidence and humanity; gaining healthier priorities and values; and treasuring their family bonds, commitments, and relationships.

The Montague Family: The Family Service Plan

Nina Montague has already been diagnosed with posttraumatic stress disorder. Initially, her therapist met with her parents, Raul and Isabel, to explain Nina's treatment plan, to answer their questions, to assist them in making an informed choice about services for their family, and to begin formulating a family service plan. Following a discussion of the available family services and resources, the parents explained their family circumstances and requested that their entire family, including the grandparents, Alberto and Carmela, and their other children, Maria and Ernesto, participate in several educational sessions designed to help them learn about posttraumatic stress disorder, its treatment, and family coping strategies.

Following these sessions, Nina's parents considered the other available services and requested the following:

- Referral to the local affiliate of NAMI to learn about their programs and services for families;
- Several sessions to design and implement home-based interventions that will complement the treatment plan and allow the family to play an active role in Nina's treatment;
- An opportunity to learn about the special education process and possible school-based interventions for Nina;
- Separate sessions for Maria and Ernesto to answer their questions and address their concerns; and
- As-needed family consultation in person or by phone to monitor Nina's progress, deal with any current issues, and support the treatment plan.

CHAPTER TWELVE

Planning for the Future

Natalie Grossman experienced her first episode of depression when she was 13. She complained of fatigue and a lack of energy, said she had great difficulty concentrating in school, and withdrew from her family, friends, and activities. At first, her parents, Janice and Aaron, thought these changes were part of normal adolescence, assuming Natalie would soon return to her "old self"—popular, lively, and enthusiastic. Instead, her dark moods worsened, and she seemed consumed with feelings of sadness, discouragement, and self-hate. Even Natalie's 16-year-old brother, Ethan, could see the dramatic change in his sister and told his parents she seemed to be a stranger to him. Janice spoke with the school guidance counselor, who made a referral to the local mental health clinic. During the evaluation, Natalie reported she sometimes heard voices that told her to kill herself. Given the concern about a possible suicide attempt and the severity and persistence of her depression, Natalie was admitted to the inpatient unit. She was released with a diagnosis of major depression with psychotic features and a recommendation for outpatient treatment consisting of cognitive-behavioral and interpersonal therapy, antidepressant medication, and antipsychotic medication for her auditory hallucinations. She met with her psychologist weekly for ther-

apy and with her psychiatrist regularly for medication moni-
toring. The school worked with Natalie and her family to
develop an Individualized Education Plan (IEP) that met her
needs and provided appropriate accommodations. Over time,
Natalie showed significant improvement. Although she contin-
ued to have episodes of depression, her symptoms were less se-
vere. Natalie did well in school and enjoyed her many friends.
But, as she and her family planned for college and the future,
they wanted to make sure she had the treatment and support
she needed.

Some adolescents who have the disorders discussed in this book will move into successful lives as adults and have no need of further services. Indeed, young people with mental illness often demonstrate a remarkable resilience as they acquire the knowledge, skills, and attitudes required for an independent adulthood. Others, like Natalie Grossman, may require continuing mental health and other supportive services as they move ahead in their lives. Still others may continue to experience significant problems that undermine their ability to attain independence in adulthood. This third group may require comprehensive long-term planning on the part of families and professionals.

As we have discussed, results of numerous long-term outcome studies indicated that a majority of people with serious mental illness recover to build meaningful, satisfying, and productive lives (Davidson et al., 2005). But, some of them do not achieve that level of recovery. In the case of long-term outcomes for schizophrenia, for example, Torrey (2006) reported that 60% of affected individuals are completely recovered or much improved, and 15% are improved but require an extensive support network. Because recovery is a continuing process, he also reported that 10-year outcomes are slightly less positive, with 50% completely recovered or much improved and 25% partially improved. For those with bipolar disorder, Torrey and Knable (2002) reported long-term outcomes that are somewhat better: 25% recover completely, and 55% to 65% recover partially. For both disorders, however, a significant minority has continuing symptoms with a poor outcome.

Our concern in this chapter is with those adolescents who do need continuing services either to support them in achieving their goals or to assist them in managing a severe and disabling mental illness. Some of these young adults may need relatively few of the services we discuss. Others may need an array of services to remain in their communities. Working closely with a team of professionals, the youth and family can determine which services are needed and develop a transition plan designed to access appropriate services and supports.

We begin with a discussion of transitional planning. Adolescents with mental illness typically receive both special education and mental health services, and those two systems will play a central role in the planning process. But, the transition from adolescence to adulthood also involves planning for independent living. Working with a transition team, the young person and family need to establish a set of realistic goals and to access the services, resources, and supports that are needed to achieve those goals. We talk about long-term planning. Finally, we return to Natalie Grossman and offer some suggestions for transitional planning.

Transitional Planning in Special Education

High school graduation often marks the beginning of adulthood as students move on to college, jobs, and their own independence. For all students, this is a time of excitement and anxiety as possibilities are simultaneously overwhelming, electrifying, and distressing. Students with mental illness encounter these same experiences, but differences exist. Students with IEPs are often given much more support in high school, and the disappearance of this support at work, college, or job training often comes as a shock. To lessen this surprise, every student with an IEP must have a transition plan.

Similar to IEPs, transition plans are coordinated by a multidisciplinary team called the *transition team*, which is headed by a transition specialist. Also similar to IEPs, transition plans are individualized and coordinate the student's high school education with the student's goals on graduating. These goals need to be realistic in terms of a student's ability, financial situation, and mental health. In addition, the transition team needs to consider whether a particular college or job site offers any supports or if it will increase a student's stress.

If a student plans to go to college, for example, the transition plan focuses on the actions a student needs to take to make it a reality. In addition to specifying each college prep course needed, the transition plan might include SAT (Scholastic Aptitude Test) prep classes, visits to local colleges, and a timeline for assembling college applications. The transition plan may also focus on developing the skills needed to succeed, such as organization, self-advocacy, self-discipline, and ability to create a support system. Without all of these elements in place, the transition may not proceed smoothly, and the success of the student might be in jeopardy. The chosen college needs to be one that does not augment a student's stress unnecessarily; for some students, a smaller college or a local college might be the best choice.

Similarly, if a student expects to secure employment after high school graduation, the transition plan should focus on helping the student obtain the skill set necessary for the job and any life skills needed to live as independently as possible. Students can gain these skills through high school courses, vocational school, and local internships. One avenue of securing assistance after high school is through the state Office of Vocational Rehabilitation (OVR). Operating under the auspices of the U.S. Labor Department's Office of Disability Employment Policy (ODEP), each state's OVR is able to provide services to eligible individuals with disabilities. Eligibility is decided within 60 days of submitting a formal request to the OVR and often includes a meeting with an OVR counselor. Services provided can include vocational counseling, on-the-job training, job placement services, and financial assistance while obtaining necessary skills. In some states, this financial assistance may include costs for college tuition or textbooks. Because of the breadth of services offered through OVR, it is recommended that an OVR representative be contacted shortly after the transition team meeting to determine if the student qualifies for services and how the school and OVR can collaborate.

Legally, a transition plan must be developed by the time the student is 16 years old (if the IEP is already in place). Due to the nature of schooling, however, we suggest that development of the transition plan begins in eighth grade so that high school courses reflect the end goals. Although parents and teachers are instrumental in developing this plan, the realistic desires and goals of the student should be the focus.

Transitional Planning in Mental Health

In 2008, the U.S. Government Accountability Office (GAO) published a report, *Young Adults With Serious Mental Illness: Some States and Federal Agencies Are Taking Steps to Address Their Transition Challenges*. The report generally used the Substance Abuse and Mental Health Services Administration (SAMHSA; 2004) definition of *serious mental illness* to refer those who are age 18 or older and have a diagnosable mental disorder that results in significant impairment in one or more functional areas, such as self-care, education, employment, or social relationships. The GAO estimated that in 2006 at least 2.4 million young adults aged 18 through 26 (6.5% of the noninstitutionalized young adults in that age range) had a serious mental illness, such as major depression, bipolar disorder, or schizophrenia. The report noted that the actual number is likely to be higher because homeless, institutionalized, and incarcerated individuals were not included in the estimate, and those groups are characterized by relatively high rates of mental illness. An additional 9.3 million (25.3%) had moderate or mild mental illness. Overall, nearly one in three young adults experienced some degree of mental illness in 2006. Among those with serious mental illness, almost 90% had more than one mental disorder.

Compared to their peers, young adults with serious mental illness had significantly lower rates of high school graduation and postsecondary education. About 186,00 young adults received Social Security Administration disability benefits in 2006 because of a mental illness that prevented them from engaging in substantial gainful employment. In fact, some individuals who are eligible for disability benefits may not have applied or completed the application process, which requires the submission of medical records that document the nature of the mental illness, the probable duration of the symptoms, and the degree of impairment the illness imposes as well as proof of income for Supplemental Security Income (SSI) eligibility. That process might prove too difficult for some people who have serious mental illness.

As the GAO report (2008) noted, although the transition to adulthood can be difficult for all young adults, it is particularly challenging for those with serious mental illness. This is a period when they need to assume greater responsibility for their independence and make critical decisions about relationships and careers that affect their future. This transition can involve completing school, securing full-time employment, becoming financially independent, establishing a residence, entering into a long-term relationship, and becoming a parent. The sound judgment and interpersonal skills most needed during this period are precisely those that can be impaired by the illness. Moreover, the severity of symptoms can vary over time, derailing their plans to complete school or begin a career. When these young adults do not succeed in transitioning to adulthood, the result can be economic hardship, social isolation, and in some cases, suicide, all of which can pose substantial costs to individuals, families, and society.

As detailed in the report (GAO, 2008), these young adults face many challenges, including:

- Difficulty finding available mental health, vocational rehabilitation, employment, life skills, and housing services that are tailored to their mental disability and age range;
- Difficulty qualifying for programs that provide or pay for mental

health services, which often have more stringent requirements for adults, thus disrupting the continuity of their treatment; and

- Difficulty navigating the multiple discrete programs and delivery systems that address their varied needs.

An additional problem is the frequent absence of adult service providers who are trained in adolescent development and prepared to work with young adults who have serious mental illness, and who tend to be relatively psychosocially immature. In response to these challenges, young adults with mental illness may choose not to participate in services.

The Bazelon Center for Mental Health Law (2004; http://www .bazelon.org/) discussed the unmet needs of transitional youth as well as the consequences of this neglect. Regarding education and employment, over 60% of these young adults are unable to complete high school, they are often unemployed, and they lack the skills necessary for independent living. Compared to their peers in the general population, these young adults are three times more likely to be involved in criminal activity, and they have higher rates of substance abuse than any other age group with mental illness. Transitional youth face an increased risk of suicide: An estimated 20% of youth receiving mental health treatment have either contemplated or attempted suicide, and fewer than 40% of youth at risk of suicide receive treatment.

Clearly, these vulnerable young adults need individualized services that can assist them with education, employment, housing, and independent living. The Bazelon Center (2004) cited the following barriers to meeting these needs: (a) gaps in child-serving services when these youth age out of special education, child welfare, and juvenile justice services; (b) underutilization of services that are available due to stigma associated with mental illness, the cost of services, and dissatisfaction with available services; and (c) lack of support necessary for managing their illness. The center's recommendations include the following: creating a comprehensive service system for youth in transition, encouraging the adult mental health system to develop programs for young adults aged 19 to 25, ensuring continued Medicaid eligibility through age 24 for youth on SSI at age 18, and providing funding to develop proven services specially designed for transitional youth.

Although comprehensive transitional planning is necessarily multi-systemic and collaborative, one specific concern is the transfer of youth from the child and adolescent mental health services to adult mental health services. As noted, some adolescents may no longer require mental health services. At the same time, such disorders as major depression, bipolar disorder, and schizophrenia are likely to persist into adulthood and require continuing care. Thus, it is important to begin to work with these young people by age 17 and to ensure continuity of mental health care. With the involvement of the adolescent and family, planning should include careful assessment of the adolescent's current and long-term needs, information regarding available services, assistance in making an informed choice regarding services, and a plan for the transfer from child to adult services.

A useful publication is *Transition to Adulthood: A Resource for Assisting Young People With Emotional or Behavioral Difficulties* (H. B. Clark & Davis, 2000). The book, which includes young adults as contributors, discusses a range of interventions that can assist these adolescents to deal with the challenges that accompany the transition to adulthood.

Long-Term Planning for Families

The focus in this section is on adults with serious mental illness who continue to experience severe and persistent impairment in multiple life areas. These individuals and their families need to establish a safety net of long-term services and support, which in turn requires long-term planning. People with significant psychiatric disability are generally eligible for a range of benefits, including Social Security Disability Insurance (SSDI), SSI, and public assistance (welfare), as well as associated health care and other benefits. Practitioners can make appropriate referrals and assist families to understand and obtain these benefits.

Community resources are an essential component of the long-term plan. A local case manager can serve as the individual's advocate, coordinate mental health and other important services, and keep the family informed about residential living arrangements available in the community. Sometimes, family members, such as parents of an adult child who resides at home, perform these functions. As they age, however, parents need to develop a community network that can meet the needs of their adult child on a continuing basis. Such a network is essential for siblings who do not reside locally.

Long-term planning also involves family resources. Families should contact a lawyer who is knowledgeable about estate planning for people with serious mental illness and who can meet regularly with the family. The family needs to ensure that long-term plans do not jeopardize eligibility for SSDI, SSI, and other benefits. For instance, if parents wish to leave money after their death without jeopardizing their adult child's eligibility for benefits, the family may wish to establish a trust fund and appoint a trustee to administer the trust. The trustee, either an individual or financial institution, distributes funds based on the specific provisions of the trust.

The family can also benefit from other resources, both locally and nationally. For example, the National Alliance on Mental Illness (NAMI; http://www.nami.org/) can provide information about the Planned Lifetime Assistance Network (PLAN), which offers continuity of care for people with mental illness. The program is based on an individualized written plan that specifies the supplementary benefits to be provided to the relative and the financial means (usually a type of trust) to pay for the service.

Natalie Grossman: Planning for the Future

As mentioned in the opening vignette, Natalie Grossman was diagnosed at age 13 with major depression. Following her hospitalization, a multidisciplinary team (MDT) was established to develop an IEP that would help her succeed academically and accomplish her long-term goals. The MDT consisted of Natalie, her parents, a social worker who provided information from her psychiatrist and psychologist, and various school personnel. As a result of her continuing treatment and school-based accommodations, Natalie showed significant improvement throughout high school. Her depressive symptoms became less frequent and severe, and she received As and Bs in her college prep courses. Since ninth grade, Natalie and her parents had been working with her IEP team to develop and implement a transition plan, which included the following objectives:

- To undertake a careful assessment of Natalie's skills in various areas as well as her current and long-term needs;
- To monitor Natalie's academic progress and mental health status;
- To schedule SAT prep classes during her junior year;
- To offer an opportunity during her senior year to take an introductory course at a local college to determine her readiness for postsecondary education;
- To evaluate alternative plans for college, such as commuting to a local college, living in a residence hall at a local college, or attending an out-of-state college or university;
- To provide information regarding available mental health services in the college setting, assistance in making an informed choice regarding services, and a plan for the transfer from child to adult services once Natalie's plans are in place;
- To make referrals to mental health providers in the college setting who can meet her continuing needs for medication and therapy; and
- To contact the college disabilities office to obtain information about available services, to provide documentation of her disability, and to determine the accommodations Natalie might need during college.

From the onset of Natalie's depression, mental health and educational professionals helped her family obtain the information, skills, and services they needed. With this support, Natalie and her parents learned to manage her illness and now face the future with hope and optimism. Working with other families of young people who have mental illness, professionals have a similar opportunity to empower these families in the present and help them prepare for the future.

References

Akiskal, H. S. (2008). The emergence of the bipolar spectrum: Validation along clinical-epidemiologic and familial-genetic lines. *Psychopharmacology Bulletin, 40*, 99–115.

American Academy of Child & Adolescent Psychiatry. (2002). *Statement from the American Academy of Child and Adolescent Psychiatry for the Senate Health, Education, Labor and Pensions Committee hearing on IDEA enforcement: April 25, 2002.* Retrieved May 25, 2008, from http://www.aacap.org/galleries/LegislativeAction/IDEASenatehrgStatement4-02.PDF

American Academy of Child & Adolescent Psychiatry. (2004a). *The continuum of care for children and adolescents.* Retrieved February 25, 2008, from http://www.aacap.org/cs/root/facts_for_families/the_continuum_of_care_for_children_and_adolescents

American Academy of Child & Adolescent Psychiatry. (2004b). *Schizophrenia in children.* Retrieved March 25, 2008, from http://www.aacap.org/cs/root/facts_for_families/schizophrenia_in_children

American Academy of Child & Adolescent Psychiatry. (2005). *Comprehensive psychiatric evaluation.* Retrieved January 3, 2008, from http://www.aacap.org/cs/root/facts_for_families/comprehensive_psychiatric_evaluation

American Academy of Child & Adolescent Psychiatry. (2008). *Teen suicide.* Retrieved February 14, 2009, from http://www.aacap.org/cs/root/facts_for_families/teen_suicide

American Academy of Pediatrics. (2004). School-based mental health services. *Pediatrics, 113*, 1839–1845.

American Association of Suicidology. (2006). *Youth suicide fact sheet.* Retrieved May 15, 2008, from http://www.suicidology.org/c/document_library/get_file?folderId=232&name=DLFE-24.pdf

American Association of Suicidology. (2007). *Facts about suicide and depression.* Retrieved May 15, 2008, from http://www.suicidology.org/c/document_library/get_file?folderId=232&name=DLFE-21.pdf

American Psychiatric Association. (2000). *Diagnostic and statistical manual of mental disorders* (4th ed., text revision). Washington, DC: Author.

Barnard, M. U. (2003). *Helping your depressed child.* Oakland, CA: New Harbinger.

Bazelon Center for Mental Health Law. (2004). *Facts on transitional services for youth with mental illnesses.* Retrieved February 15, 2009, from http://www.bazelon.org/issues/children/factsheets/transition.htm

Beavers, R. W., & Hampson, R. B. (1990). *Successful families: Assessment and intervention.* New York: Norton.

Bourne, E. J. (2005). *The anxiety & phobia workbook* (4th ed.). Oakland, CA: New Harbinger.

Brozovich, R., & Chase, L. (2008). *Say goodbye to being shy: A workbook to help kids overcome shyness.* Oakland, CA: New Harbinger.

Canadian Mental Health Association. (2004) *Mental health and high school: A guide for students.* Retrieved May 27, 2008, from http://www.cmha.ca/highschool

Centers for Disease Control and Prevention. (2007a). *Suicide prevention.* Retrieved January 21, 2008, from http://www.cdc.gov/ncipc/dvp/suicide/

Centers for Disease Control and Prevention. (2007b). *Suicide trends among youths and young adults aged 10-24 years—United States, 1900-2004.* Retrieved January 14, 2008, from http://www.cdc.gov/mmwr/preview/mmwrhtml/mm5635a2.htm

Chansky, T. E. (2000). *Freeing your child from obsessive-compulsive disorder.* New York: Three Rivers Press.

Chansky, T. E. (2004). *Freeing your child from anxiety.* New York: Broadway Books.

Clark, H. B., & Davis, M. (Eds.). (2000). *Transition to adulthood: A resource for assisting young people with emotional or behavioral difficulties.* Baltimore, MD: Brookes.

Clark, M. D. (2008). *Our vision: "To realize a helping field where strengths are the standard."* Retrieved February 5, 2008, from http://www.buildmotivation.com/

Cobain, B. (2007). *When nothing matters anymore: A survival guide for depressed teens.* Minneapolis, MN: Free Spirit.

Cook-Morales, V. J. (2002) The home-school-agency triangle. In D. T. Marsh & M. A. Fristad (Eds.), *Handbook of serious emotional disturbance in children and adolescents* (pp. 392–411). New York: Wiley.

Copeland, M. E. (2001). *The depression workbook: A guide for living with depression and manic depression* (2nd ed.). Oakland, CA: New Harbinger.

Copeland, M. E., & Copans, S. (2002). *Recovering from depression.: A workbook for teens* (Rev. ed.). Baltimore: Brookes.

Crist, J. J. (2004). *What to do when you're scared & worried.* Minneapolis, MN: Free Spirit.

Davidson, L., Harding, C., & Spaniol, L. (Eds.). (2005). *Recovery from severe mental illnesses: Research evidence and implications for practice* (Vol. 1). Boston: Boston University Center for Psychiatric Rehabilitation.

Davis, M., Eshelman, E. R., & McKay, M. (2006). *Relaxation & stress reduction workbook* (5th ed.). Oakland, CA: New Harbinger.

Dixon, L., Adams, C., & Lucksted, A. (2000). Update on family psychoeducation for schizophrenia. *Schizophrenia Bulletin, 26,* 5–20.

Dixon, L., McFarlane, W. R., Lefley, H., Lucksted, A., Cohen, M., Falloon, I., et al. (2001). Evidence-based practices for services to families of people with psychiatric disabilities. *Psychiatric Services, 52,* 903–910.

Dixon, L., Stewart, B., Burland, J., Delahanty, J., Lucksted, A., & Hoffman, M. (2001). Pilot study of the effectiveness of the Family-to-Family Education Program. *Psychiatric Services, 52,* 965–967.

Dunst, C. J., Trivette, C. M., & Deal, A. G. (Eds.). (1994). *Strengthening and supporting families. Volume 1: Methods, strategies and practices.* Cambridge, MA: Brookline.

Eisen, A. R., & Engler, L. B. (2006). *Helping your child overcome separation anxiety or school refusal: A step-by-step guide for parents.* Oakland, CA: New Harbinger.

Faedda, G. L., & Austin, N. B. (2006). *Parenting a bipolar disorder: What to do and why.* Oakland, CA: New Harbinger.

Families and Advocates Partnership for Education. (2004). *IDEA 2004 Summary.* Retrieved May 28, 2008, from http://www.fape.org/idea/2004/summary.htm

Fewell, R. R. (1986). A handicapped child in the family. In R. R. Fewell & P. F. Vadasy (Eds.), *Families of handicapped children: Needs and supports across the life span* (pp. 3–34). Austin, TX: Pro-Ed.

Figley, C. R. (1989). *Helping traumatized families.* San Francisco: Jossey-Bass.

Finley, L. (1997). The multiple effects of culture and ethnicity on psychiatric disability. In L. Spaniol, C. Gagne, & M. Koehler (Eds.), *Psychological and social aspects of psychiatric disability* (pp. 497–510). Boston: Boston University Center for Psychiatric Rehabilitation.

Fitch, B. (1994). Through a glass darkly. *The Journal of NAMI California, 5*(4), 37–40.

Fitzgibbons, L., & Pedrick, C. (2003). *Helping your child with OCD.* Oakland, CA: New Harbinger.

Foa, E. B., & Andrews, L. W. (2006). *If your adolescent has an anxiety disorder: An essential resource for parents.* New York: Oxford University Press.

Fristad, M. A., & Arnold, J. S. G. (2004). *Raising a moody child: How to cope with depression and bipolar disorder*. New York: Guilford.

Fristad, M. A., Shaver, A. E., & Holderle, K. E. (2002). Mood disorders in childhood and adolescence. In D. T. Marsh & M. A. Fristad (Eds.), *Handbook of serious emotional disturbance in children and adolescents* (pp. 228–265). New York: Wiley.

Goode, E. E. (1989, April 24). When mental illness hits home. *U.S. News & World Report*, pp. 55–57, 60, 62–65.

Greenberg, M. (2008). *Hurry down sunshine*. New York: Other Press.

Greenberg, R. (2007). *Bipolar kids: Helping your child find calm in the mood storm*. Cambridge, MA: Da Capo Press.

Gruttadaro, D., Burns, B. J., Duckworth, K., & Crudo, D. (2007). *Choosing the right treatment: What families need to know about evidence-based practices*. Arlington, VA: National Alliance on Mental Illness (NAMI).

Gur, R. E., & Johnson, A. B. (2006). *If your adolescent has schizophrenia: An essential resource for parents*. New York: Oxford University Press.

Hansen, M., Anderson, C., Gray, C., Harbaugh, S., Lindblad-Goldberg, M., & Marsh, D.T. (1999). *Child, family and community core competencies*. Harrisburg: Pennsylvania Child and Adolescent Service System Program Training and Technical Assistance Institute.

Haugaard, J. J. (2008). *Child psychopathology*. New York: McGraw-Hill.

Hawkins, P., & Hawkins, R. (2000). A mother and daughter share their experiences. *The Journal of NAMI California, 11*(1), 11–13.

Herbert, B. (2005). *My bipolar, roller coaster, feelings book*. Victoria, BC, Canada: Trafford.

Heubner, D. (2006). *What to do when you worry too much: A kid's guide to overcoming anxiety*. Washington, DC: Magination Press.

Hyman, B. M., & Pedrick, C. (2005). *The OCD workbook* (2nd ed.). Oakland, CA: New Harbinger.

Jackson-Triche, M., Wells, K. B., & Minnium, K. (2002). *Beating depression: The journey to hope.* New York: McGraw-Hill.

Jamison, K. R. (1995). *An unquiet mind: A memoir of moods and madness.* New York: Knopf.

Jamison, K. R. (1996). *Touched with fire: Manic-depressive illness and the artistic temperament.* New York: Free Press.

Jans, L., Stoddard, S., & Kraus, L. (2004). *Chartbook on mental health and disability in the United States* (an InfoUse Report). Washington, DC: U.S. Department of Education, National Institute on Disability and Rehabilitation Research.

Johnson, E., Mellard, D. F., Fuchs, D., & McKnight, M. A. (2006). *Responsiveness to intervention (RTI): How to do it.* Lawrence, KS: National Research Center on Learning Disabilities.

Kazdin, A. E. (2008a). Ensuring that our findings have impact. *Monitor on Psychology, 39*(2), 5.

Kazdin, A. E. (2008b). Evidence-based treatment and practice: New opportunities to bridge clinical research and practice, enhance the knowledge base, and improve patient care. *American Psychologist, 63*, 146–159.

Kazdin, A. E., Stolar, M. J., & Marciano, P. L. (1995). Risk factors for dropping out of treatment among white and black families. *Journal of Family Psychology, 9*, 402–417.

Kelley, W. (1992). Unmet needs. *The Journal of the California Alliance for the Mentally Ill, 3*(1), 28.

Kuipers, L., Birchwood, M., & McCreadie, R. G. (2002). Psychosocial family intervention in schizophrenia: A review of empirical studies. *British Journal of Psychiatry, 160*, 272–275.

Kutash, K., Duchnowski, A. J., & Lynn, N. (2006). *School-based mental health: An empirical guide for decision-makers.* Tampa: University of South Florida, Louis de la Parte Florida Mental Health Institute, Department of Child and Family Studies, Research and Training Center for Children's Mental Health.

Lederman, J., & Fink, C. (2003). *The ups and downs of raising a bipolar child: A survival guide for parents.* New York: Fireside.

Lefley, H. P. (1996). *Family caregiving in mental illness* (Family Caregiver Applications Series, Vol. 7). Thousand Oaks, CA: Sage.

Lefley, H. P. (1998). The family experience in cultural context: Implications for further research and practice. *New Directions for Mental Health Services, 77,* 97–106.

Lombardo, G. T. (2006). *Understanding the mind of your bipolar child.* New York: St. Martin's Griffen.

Marsh, D. T. (1992). *Families and mental illness: New directions in professional practice.* New York: Praeger.

Marsh, D. T. (1998). *Serious mental illness and the family: The practitioner's guide.* New York: Wiley.

Marsh, D. T. (2001). *A family-focused approach to serious mental illness: Empirically supported interventions.* Sarasota, FL: Professional Resource Press.

Marsh, D. T., & Dickens, R. M. (1997). *Troubled journey: Coming to terms with the mental illness of a sibling or parent.* New York: Tarcher/Putnam.

Marsh, D. T., & Fristad, M. A. (Eds.). (2002). *Handbook of serious emotional disturbance in children and adolescents.* New York: Wiley.

Marsh, D. T., Koeske, R. D., & Schultz, K. (1993). Services for families: A NAMI CAN Survey. *Innovations & Research, 2*(4), 53–54.

Marsh, D. T., & Lefley, H. P. (2003). Family interventions for schizophrenia. *Journal of Family Psychotherapy, 14,* 47–67.

Marsh, D. T., & Lefley, H. P. (2009). Serious mental illness: Family experiences, needs, and interventions. In J. H. Bray & M. Stanton (Eds.), *Blackwell handbook of family psychology* (pp. 742–754). Oxford, UK: Wiley-Blackwell.

Marsh, D. T., Lefley, H. P., Evans-Rhodes, D., Ansell, V. I., Doerzbacher, B. M., LaBarbera, L., et al. (1996). The family experience of mental illness: Evidence for resilience. *Psychiatric Rehabilitation Journal, 20*(2), 3–12.

Martin, J. (2000). Caught between a rock and a hard place: How the school failed me. *The Journal of NAMI California, 11*(1), 8–10.

Massie, J. (2000). A family's experience with hospitalization. *The Journal of NAMI California, 11*(1), 24–25.

McCarthy, A. M., Kelly, M. W., & Reed, D. (2000). Medication administration practices of school nurses. *Journal of School Health, 70*, 371–376.

McCubbin, H. I., & McCubbin, M. A. (1988). Typologies of resilient families: Emerging roles of social class and ethnicity. *Family Relations, 37*, 247–254.

McFarlane, W. R., Hornby, H., Dixon, L., & McNary, S. (2002). Psychoeducational multifamily groups: Research and implementation in the United States. In H. P. Lefley & D. L. Johnson (Eds.), *Family interventions in mental illness: International perspectives* (pp. 43–60). Westport, CT: Praeger.

McKay, M., Davis, M., & Fanning, P. (1995). *Messages: The communication skills book* (2nd ed.). Oakland, CA: New Harbinger.

McKay, M., & Fanning, P. (2002). *Successful problem solving.* Oakland, CA: New Harbinger.

Miklowitz, D. J. (2002). *The bipolar disorder survival guide.* New York: Guilford.

Miklowitz, D. J., & George, E. L. (2008). *The bipolar teen: What you can do to help your child and your family.* New York: Guilford.

Miklowitz, D. J., & Otto, M. W. (2008). Psychosocial interventions for bipolar disorder: A review of literature and introduction of the Systematic Treatment Enhancement Program. *Psychopharmacology Bulletin, 40*, 116–131.

Miklowitz, D. J., Simoneau, T. L., George, E. L., Richards, J. A., Kalbag, A., Sachs-Ericsson, N., et al. (2002). Family-focused treatment of bipolar disorder: One-year effects of a psychoeducational program in conjunction with pharmacotherapy. *Biological Psychiatry, 48*, 582–592.

Moltz, D. A. (1993). Bipolar disorder and the family: An integrative model. *Family Process, 32*, 409–423.

Mondimore, F. M. (2002). *Adolescent depression: A guide for parents.* Baltimore: Johns Hopkins University Press.

Morey, B., & Mueser, K. T. (2007). *The family intervention guide to mental illness.* Oakland, CA: New Harbinger.

Mowbray, C. T., Megivern, D., & Strauss, S. (2002). College students' narratives of high school experiences: Coping with serious emotional disturbance. In D. T. Marsh & M. A. Fristad (Eds.), *Handbook of serious emotional disturbance in children and adolescents* (pp. 14-29). New York: Wiley.

Mueser, K. T., & Gingerich, S. (2006). *The complete family guide to schizophrenia.* New York: Guilford.

Mueser, K. T., & Glynn, S. M. (1999). *Behavioral family therapy for psychiatric disorders* (2nd ed.). Oakland, CA: New Harbinger.

Mueser, K. T., Torrey, W. C., Lynde, D., Singer, P., & Drake, R. E. (2003). Implementing evidence-based practices for people with severe mental illness. *Behavior Modification, 27,* 387-411.

National Alliance on Mental Illness. (1999). *Families on the brink: The impact of ignoring children with serious mental illness—Results of a national survey of parents and other caregivers.* Arlington, VA: Author.

National Federation of Families for Children's Mental Health. (2008). *Working definition of family-driven care.* Retrieved February 14, 2009, from http://www.ffcmh.org/

National Institute of Mental Health. (2000). *Treatment of children with mental disorders* (NIH Publication No. 00-4702). Bethesda, MD: National Institute of Mental Health, National Institutes of Health, U.S. Department of Health and Human Services.

National Institute of Mental Health. (2007). *NIMH perspective on diagnosing and treating bipolar disorder in children.* Retrieved January 21, 2008, from http://www.nimh.nih.gov/

National Institute of Mental Health. (2008). *Antidepressant medication for children and adolescents: Information for parents and caregivers.* Retrieved January 21, 2008, from http://www.nimh.nih.gov/

New America Foundation. (2007). *Educational Policy Program: Federal funding—Individuals with Disabilities Education Act.*

Retrieved May 28, 2008, from http://www.newamerica.net/ programs/education_policy/federal_education_budget_project/ idea/federal_funding

New Freedom Commission on Mental Health. (2003). *Achieving the promise: Transforming mental health care in America. Final Report* (DHHS Pub. No. SMA-03-3832). Rockville, MD: Author.

Oster, G. D., & Montgomery, S. S. (1995). *Helping your depressed teenager.* New York: Wiley.

Papolos, D., & Papols, J. (2006). *The bipolar child* (3rd ed.). New York: Broadway Books.

Paterson, R. J. (2000). *The assertiveness workbook.* Oakland, CA: New Harbinger.

Petska, S. (2006). IDEA 2004: *Significant changes in special education law effective July 1, 2005—Interim guidance (memo).* State of Wisconsin Department of Public Instruction. Retrieved May 28, 2008, from dpi.wi.gov/sped/doc/idea04change.doc

Physicians' Desk Reference (63rd edition). (2008). New York: Thompson Reuters.

Pires, S. A. (2002). *Building systems of care: A primer.* Washington, DC: National Technical Assistance Center for Children's Mental Health, Center for Child Health and Mental Health Policy, Georgetown University Child Development Center.

Rando, T. A. (Ed.). (1986). *Parental loss of a child.* Champaign, IL: Research Press.

Rapee, R. M., Spence, S. H., Cobham, V., & Wignall, A. (2000). *Helping your anxious child: A step-by-step guide for parents.* Oakland, CA: New Harbinger.

Richards, D. M. (1999). *Overview of 504.* Council of Educators for Students with Disabilities. Retrieved May 28, 2008, from http:// www.504idea.org/504overview.html

Ringeisen, H., & Hoagwood, K. (2002). Clinical and research directions for the treatment and delivery of children's mental health services. In D. T. Marsh & M. A. Fristad (Eds.), *Handbook of serious emotional disturbance in children and adolescents* (pp. 33–55). New York: Wiley.

Roberts, M. C., Carlson, C. I., Erickson, M. T., Friedman, R. M., La Greca, A. M., Lemanek, K. L., et al. (1998). A model for training psychologists to provide services for children and adolescents. *Professional Psychology: Research and Practice, 29,* 293–299.

Rolland, J. S. (1994). *Families, illness, and disability: An integrative treatment model.* New York: Basic Books.

Rosenbaum, J., F., & Covino, J. M. (2008). Treatment of child and adolescent depression. Retrieved July 9, 2008, from http://www.medscape.com/viewarticle/576518?src=mp&spon=12&uac=53565HR

Rubin, N. J., Bebeau, M., Leigh, I. W., Lichtenberg, J. W., Nelson, P. D., Portnoy, S., et al. (2007). The competency movement within psychology: An historical perspective. *Professional Psychology: Research and Practice, 38,* 452–462.

Saks, E. R. (2007). *The center cannot hold.* New York: Hyperion.

Schab, L. M. (2008). *The anxiety workbook for teens.* Oakland, CA: New Harbinger.

Schumacher, J. (2008, July 6). A support group is my higher power. *The New York Times,* Sunday Styles, p. 6.

Seligman, M. E. (2006). *Learned optimism.* New York: Vintage Books.

Seligman, M., & Darling, R. B. (2007). *Ordinary families, special children: A systems approach to childhood disability* (3rd ed.). New York: Guilford.

Sisemore, T. A. (2007). *I bet I won't fret: A workbook to help children with generalized anxiety disorder.* Oakland, CA: New Harbinger.

Spaniol, L., & Zipple, A. M. (1997). The family recovery process. In L. Spaniol, C. Gagne, & M. Koehler (Eds.), *Psychological and social aspects of psychiatric disability* (pp. 281–284). Boston: Boston University Center for Psychiatric Rehabilitation.

Spencer, E. D., DuPont, R. L., & DuPont, C. M. (2003). *The anxiety cure for kids: A guide for parents.* New York: Wiley.

Styron, W. (1990). *Darkness visible: A memoir of madness.* New York: Random House.

Substance Abuse and Mental Health Services Administration. (2003). *Children and adolescents with anxiety disorders.* Retrieved May 5, 2008, from http://mentalhealth.samhsa.gov/publications/allpubs/ca-0007/default.asp

Substance Abuse and Mental Health Services Administration. (2004). *Serious mental illness and its co-occurrence with substance use disorders, 2002.* Retrieved February 14, 2009, at http://www.oas.samhsa.gov/CoD/Cod.htm

Substance Abuse and Mental Health Services Administration. (2005). *Family guide to systems of care for children with mental health needs.* Retrieved November 21, 2008, from http://mentalhealth.samhsa.gov/publications/allpubs/Ca-0029/default.asp

Substance Abuse and Mental Health Services Administration. (2007). *Systems of care.* Retrieved February 26, 2008, at http://systemsofcare.samhsa.gov/

Taylor, S. E., Klein, L. C., Lewis, B. P., Gruenewald, T. L., Gurung, R. A. R., & Updegraff, J. A. (2000). Biobehavioral responses to stress in females: Tend-and-befriend, not fight-or-flight. *Psychological Review, 107,* 411–429.

Torrey, E. F. (2006). *Surviving schizophrenia: A manual for families, consumers, and providers* (5th ed.). New York: HarperCollins.

Torrey, E. F., & Knable, M. B. (2002). *Surviving manic depression: A manual on bipolar disorder for patients, families and providers.* New York: Basic Books.

U.S. Department of Civil Rights. (2005). *Protecting students with disabilities.* Chicago Office of the Office of Civil Rights. Retrieved May 27, 2008, from http://www.ed.gov/about/offices/list/ocr/504faq.html

U.S. Department of Education. (2005). *27th Annual Report to Congress on the implementation of the Individuals With Disabilities Education Act, vol. 1.* Prepared by Westat for the Office of Special Education and Rehabilitative Services, U.S. Department of Education. Retrieved May 27, 2008, from http://www.ed.gov/about/reports/annual/osep/2005/index.html

U.S. Department of Education. (2006). *Building the legacy: IDEA 2004.* Office of Special Education and Rehabilitative Services, Department of Education. Retrieved May 25, 2008, from http://idea.ed.gov/explore/view/p/%2Croot%2Cregs%2C

U.S. Department of Education. (2007a). *Archived: A 25 year history of the IDEA: History—Twenty-five years of progress in educating children with disabilities through IDEA.* Retrieved May 28, 2008, from http://www.ed.gov/policy/speced/leg/idea/history.html

U.S. Department of Education. (2007b). *Archived information: A guide to the Individualized Education Program.* Office of Special Education and Rehabilitative Services. Retrieved June 4, 2008, from http://www.ed.gov/parents/needs/speced/iepguide/index.html

U.S. Department of Education. (2007c). *Family Educational Rights and Privacy Act (FERPA).* Retrieved June 24, 2008, from http://www.ed.gov/policy/gen/guid/fpco/ferpa/index.html

U.S. Department of Health and Human Services. (1999). *Mental health: A report of the surgeon general.* Washington, DC: Author.

U.S. Department of Health and Human Services. (2000). *Report of the Surgeon General's Conference on Children's Mental Health: A national action agenda.* Washington, DC: Author.

U.S. Department of Health and Human Services. (2008). *Your rights under Section 504 of the Rehabilitation Act.* Office for Civil Rights. Retrieved on May 27, 2008, from http://www.hhs.gov/ocr/504.html

U.S. General Accounting Office. (2008). *Young adults with serious mental illness: Some states and federal agencies are taking steps to address their transition challenges* (Publication No. GAO-08-678). Washington, DC: Author.

Verduzco, A. (2000). A teenager's perspective on having a mental disorder. *The Journal of NAMI California, 11*(1), 17–20.

Volkmar, F. R., & Tsatsanis, K. (2002). Psychosis and psychotic conditions in childhood and adolescence. In D. T. Marsh & M. A. Fristad (Eds.), *Handbook of serious emotional disturbance in children and adolescents* (pp. 266-283). New York: Wiley.

Wagner, A. P. (2002a). *What to do when your child has obsessive-compulsive disorder: Strategies and solutions.* Rochester, NY: Lighthouse Press.

Wagner, A. P. (2002b). *Worried no more: Help and hope for anxious children.* Rochester, NY: Lighthouse Press.

Wagner, A. P., & Jutton, P. A. (2004). *Up and down the worry hill: A children's book about obsessive-compulsive disorder and its treatment.* Rochester, NY: Lighthouse Press.

Walsh, F. (2006). *Strengthening family resilience* (2nd ed.). New York: Guilford.

Waters, D. B., & Lawrence, E. C. (1993). *Competence, courage, and change: An approach to family therapy.* New York: Norton.

Watson, W. H. (2007). From the president: In praise of magic. *Family Psychologist, 23*(4), 1, 45-46.

Weisburd, S. B. (1992). Adapting to the changed relationship: One sibling's perspective. *The Journal of the California Alliance for the Mentally Ill, 3*(1), 13-15.

World Health Organization. (2001). *The world health report.* Retrieved February 14, 2009, from http://www.who.int/whr/2001/chapter2/

Yell, M. L. (2006). *The law and special education.* Upper Saddle River, NJ: Pearson.

Youngstrom, E. A., Birmaher, B., & Findling, R. L. (2008). *Pediatric bipolar disorder: Validity, phenomenology, and recommendations for diagnosis.* Retrieved May 14, 2008, from http://www.medscape.com/medline/abstract/18199237?prt=true

Index